SHOUT YOUR ABORTION

SHOUT YOUR ABORTION

FOREWORD BY **LINDY WEST**

EDITED BY **AMELIA BONOW** & **EMILY NOKES**

SHOUT YOUR ABORTION
Edited by Amelia Bonow and Emily Nokes
Foreword by Lindy West

Cover, book design, and layout by Emily Nokes.

PM Press
PO Box 23912
Oakland, CA 94623
www.pmpress.org

ISBN: 978-1-62963-573-6
Library of Congress Control Number: 2018931525

Printed by the Employee Owners of Thomson-Shore in Dexter, Michigan
www.thomsonshore.com

Canadian publishing: Between the Lines
401 Richmond Street West, Studio 277, Toronto, Ontario, M5V 3A8, Canada
1–800–718–7201 | www.btlbooks.com

978-1-77113-383-8	Between the Lines book
978-1-77113-384-5	Between the Lines epub
978-1-77113-385-2	Between the Lines pdf

Canadian cataloguing information is available from Library and Archives Canada

A note on the language used in this book:

This book is a feminist project intended to amplify the voices of people who have had abortions. All sorts of people have abortions, and plenty of people who have abortions do not identify as women.

We strive to use gender-neutral language when possible, and we also believe that allowing people to describe their lives on their own terms is the best way to ensure that stories are widely accessible. This book contains stories from cisgender women as well as trans and gender-nonconforming folks. Each contributor used their own language, and in some instances this includes referring to people who can have abortions as "women." There are also instances where female signifiers are used in the Foreword, Preface, and Resources.

Framing gender in terms of women and men doesn't reflect the whole reality; gender is not binary. Abortion is not simply a women's issue, it is a universal human rights issue. We look forward to building a future in which our collective language includes and respects gender-nonconforming people, and we encourage readers who wish to expand their understanding of gender to visit https://genderspectrum.org, and the World Professional Association of Transgender Health in the Resources section.

Many of the stories in the Shouts section of this book include descriptions of abortion. Some stories include references to sexual violence and abuse. We believe these stories need to be told, and we hope that readers engage with this material with an appropriate level of caution. In the words of Dr. Willie Parker, we believe that the truth will do.

ABORTION
IS
NORMAL

FOREWORD

by LINDY WEST

In September 2010 I took one pill, then another, and lay in my bed for a night and a day, and then I wasn't pregnant anymore. It was a fairly smooth experience, distressing only because my relationship was bad and I had no money. The procedure itself was an unqualified relief.

I know that's startling for some people to hear—we are conditioned to speak about abortion with reverence and a bit of melancholy, if we speak about it at all. But feeling relieved after my abortion didn't make me part of some radical vanguard, it made me utterly mundane. A full 95 percent of people who have abortions report feeling that they made the right decision. My relief didn't just place me in a majority; it placed me in a super-majority. I am part of the 95 percent. And 95 percent, as any fifth-grader can tell you, rounds up to pretty much everyone.

Abortion is normal. Abortion is common. Abortion is happening. Abortion is a necessary medical procedure. Abortion makes people's lives better. Abortion needs to be legal, safe, and accessible to everyone. Abortion is a thing you can say out loud.

That's not to say that stories more complex or painful than my own—stories of trauma, of abuse, of malpractice, of confusion, of impossible decisions—are unimportant. They are real, valid, vital threads in the vast tapestry of human experience. The fact that abortion stories are not a monolith is an indication, surely, that abortion shouldn't be treated like one. We cannot legislate away regret; all we can do is empower every human being to make informed, sovereign decisions over their own lives.

There's a reason why rape is a tool of war. When you take away a community's ability to control reproduction, you take away its ability to conserve resources, to act instead of react, to focus on building for the greater good (the future) rather than scrabbling to sustain new life (the present). On an individual level, those who are forced to bear children are denied the ability to lead self-determined, fully realized lives. Rape is a weapon of mass destruction because forced birth obliterates the notion of freedom.

At the time of this writing, abortion has been legal in America for 45 years, and one in four people who can become pregnant will have an abortion at some point in their lives. Contrary to what the pundit economy would have you believe, abortion is not particularly controversial. According to the Pew Research Center, nearly 70 percent of all Americans oppose overturning *Roe v. Wade*, while 75 percent of Democrats believe abortion should be legal in all or most cases. These are not numbers that indicate controversy.

And yet, in spite of those numbers, abortion bans and restrictions have been shuttering clinics at an unprecedented rate, leaving seven states with only one clinic, and 90 percent of counties in America with none. Regardless of legality, access to abortion simply does not exist for millions of Americans. Beyond that, with the Trump administration poised to confirm their second Supreme Court justice, the right to abortion as guaranteed by *Roe v. Wade* is set to be obliterated.

How did we find ourselves in a place where abortion access is being regulated in a way that is so profoundly out of step with public opinion? The answer is relatively simple: those who oppose abortion rights have dominated the conversation by framing abortion as murder. The Left has never figured out a compelling way to advocate for abortion rights, because the anti-choice movement has relentlessly flooded the discursive field with so much propaganda that even those who support abortion rights often do so from an apologetic stance. Those seeking to regulate reproductive freedom have intentionally created a cultural climate where talking openly about having had an abortion is a liability that most people are understandably unwilling to accept.

We cannot effectively advocate for abortion in the abstract. Abortion is good for women, families, and communities, and the proof is reflected in our own lives. Many of us have our careers or our children because of our abortions. Some of us would have never survived our abusers or our addictions without our abortions. One in four of us have had lives that were determined in monumental ways by our abortions, and the vast majority of us do not regret our decisions. But if nobody will admit they've had an abortion, we aren't able to illustrate the connection between having an abortion and living a better life.

We have to keep pushing these conversations outside of liberal urban centers and social media silos. During the great post-2016-election blame game I read an article in *Vox* called "Everything Mattered" by a writer named David Roberts. He argued that, in the midst of all the fog, resentment, and disinformation, there was one undeniable defining factor behind Donald Trump's "win": entrenched partisanship. About 90 percent of self-identified Republicans voted Republican, and 89 percent of Democrats voted Democrat. People voted for Trump against their interests, against their better judgment, against their values.

Roberts wrote: *Clinton bet most of her chips on there being some floor, some violation of norms too low even for today's radicalized Republican Party. She thought responsible Republican officeholders would rally. She thought at least well-off, well-educated Republican women would recoil in horror. She was wrong. There is no floor. Partisanship has been revealed as the strongest force in US public life—stronger than any norms, independent of any facts.*

But here's the thing: Abortion as a liberal issue is not exactly truth—it's branding. Abortion as a "debate" is not truth—it's branding. We know, because care providers know, that Democrats have abortions, Republicans have abortions, rich women have abortions, poor women have abortions, women of faith, women with children, anti-choice women, rural women, suburban women, women in cities, the proverbial white working-class women. Trans men have abortions, and gender-nonconforming people have abortions. It seems counterintuitive, but I believe abortion has the potential to be one of our most unifying issues. It cuts through all of those boundaries: race, class, geography, religion. The key is to drag abortion out of that partisan framework entirely.

Under the Obama administration we had the luxury of a more nuanced conversation. We could say, "Abortion is normal." Going forward we need to say, "Abortion is freedom." Abortion is two incomes instead of one for your struggling family. Abortion is family values. Abortion is fiscal responsibility. Abortion is liberty. Anti-choice legislation is a form of unconstitutional government intervention that undermines personal freedom.

This country is ours just like our bodies are ours. Telling our abortion stories is a form of resistance.

Without abortion we are not free. We need to work to build a culture in which talking about abortion becomes as normal as the procedure itself. Then we can begin to communicate the truth to the people in our lives who don't yet understand what we already know: People who have abortions are good people, and abortion has helped millions of us live our best lives.

We are not sorry. ■

S Y A

PREFACE

by AMELIA BONOW

Hi guys! About a year ago, I had an abortion at the Planned Parenthood on Madison Avenue in Seattle, and I remember this experience with a nearly inexpressible level of gratitude.

That's the beginning of a Facebook post I wrote about my abortion in 2015. This post catalyzed an unprecedented flash flood of abortion stories, the kind of flood that changes the surface of the earth forever. A lot has changed since then. Before I tell you how that post came to be, I'm going to tell you about Shout Your Abortion. These are the three words that Lindy West attached to my post to summarize its ethos, which now encapsulate a movement of the same name, the movement that generated this book.

Shout Your Abortion stems from the idea that abortion is normal and we are allowed to talk about our abortions however we want. This movement comprises countless individuals who are not unified by a specific political ideology or adherence to one particular strategy. We are writing graffiti in bathrooms and we are writing symphonies and we are writing jokes. We are starting group texts and we are proposing a toast at the dinner party. We are every kind of person, and our abortions felt every single kind of way. We are telling the truth about our lives and, in doing so, we are destroying the expectation of silence. We are not telling anyone else how they should feel or how they should talk about it; we are saying, *This is how it felt for me. Can you imagine?*

Abortion has been a normal part of reproductive life since the beginning of time. Why wouldn't it be? It's easy to get pregnant, it's very difficult to raise a baby, and terminating a pregnancy is generally not risky or complicated. One in four women in America have at least one abortion at some point in their lives. Having an abortion is significantly more common than having braces, getting breast cancer, or struggling with infertility. The people having these abortions are the people in your life; the fact that so many of us have never talked about abortion with somebody who has had one is nothing short of astounding.

Then again, this society represses everything. We are shaped by all sorts of things we're not supposed to talk about, and not talking about any of it has made us sick. When we don't talk about the things we've been through, our lives don't necessarily make sense, to ourselves or to other people. When nobody talks about these things, our perception as a culture becomes warped. Without real human touchstones, situations that we haven't experienced ourselves become unimaginable. People do not find empathy in a theoretical exercise.

SYA is about much more than abortion; it's about unlearning the idea that we are not supposed to talk about the things that happen to us. Part of the reason the taboo surrounding abortion is so strong is that it often touches so many other forbidden subjects: sexual violence, mental illness, poverty, addiction, incest, abuse. Our abortions are connected to all of these things, just as they're connected to our careers, our families, our health, our greatest aspirations, and our broken hearts. This book contains abortion stories from 45 individuals, but they are so much more than that. They are stories of 45 people who are telling you about the things that they've survived in order to become exactly who they are.

Regardless of context, the words *Shout Your Abortion* act as a conduit simply because they communicate that this conversation is happening. I wear the word "ABORTION" on my body most days. Most days that I do, strangers tell me about their abortions, their mothers' abortions, or the abortions had by their wives and girlfriends. I've had these exchanges with grocery store checkers, baristas, and dozens of Lyft drivers. It's happened in less than 30 seconds in an elevator and more than a handful of times during a bikini wax. Multiple times when I was walking down the street in a particularly loud T-shirt, strangers have stopped their cars next to me to ask how to find this conversation. I hope that this book is able to help people find a way in.

I hope that this book introduces people to the voices of abortion care providers, who I believe are the very best that people can be. I hope that this book inspires readers to start talking about abortion in their own lives, at whatever volume they choose, in an infinite number of ways. I hope that this book illustrates change in a way that makes people feel hopeful. Above all, I hope that this book gives people permission to love themselves—people who might have never known that was an option.

Shout Your Abortion is not a directive or a political imperative. The last thing I want is for people to feel some sense of external pressure to talk about their abortions. I don't believe that speaking out is a better or more righteous path, I simply believe that we'd all be better off if conversations about abortion were normalized. For some, speaking publicly about their abortions would be unsafe, traumatic, or just not worth it for any number of reasons. SYA was started by white women from middle-class families in the most liberal part of the country; we knew we weren't jeopardizing our most important relationships or acceptance in our communities when we decided to speak. Our bravery is a product of privilege, and having been able to access and afford our abortions is a privilege in and of itself. We hope to weaponize this privilege in a way that makes the world kinder and more just for everyone, and we hope that those who don't shout may still find healing and solidarity in the stories of others.

SYA is grateful to be building on the work of previous generations of activists and organizers who fought for our reproductive freedom. SYA functions in support of the people and organizations working on the ground to provide abortions and expand abortion access, take our legislative fights to the highest courts, and fight for a truly inclusive movement. SYA works in solidarity with the movement for reproductive justice, a movement created by activist women of color to address how race, gender, class, ability, nationality, and sexuality intersect in the fight to end reproductive oppression. Loretta Ross, one of the 12 women who founded the reproductive justice movement, said that fighting for choice is insufficient; we must fight for justice. Most people shouting their abortions are people who had a choice. It is our imperative to fight for justice.

I worry that this is a terrible, audacious time to write a book. It feels like culture, language, and objective truth are dying a million deaths a day. We're in the midst of destroying old ways of doing things as we scramble to come up with new ones, and sometimes the new ways we come up with feel outmoded six months after they're conceived. Reproductive autonomy is currently a privilege and by no means a guarantee. I don't know if we'll even have the illusion of abortion rights this time next year. But I do know that we won't see reproductive freedom until we start talking about abortion.

If we do not tell our own stories, we give other people the power to define us. The anti-choice movement terrorized us into silence decades ago, and they filled that silence with lies. But they've lost their grip. Every single day, more of us are choosing to tell the truth about our own lives. Abortion helps people live better, and good people have abortions.

We are the proof. ■

FORMATION

things started coming together

INTRODUCTION

by AMELIA BONOW

This is the story of how Shout Your Abortion began.

Like most women, I grew up fearing unwanted pregnancy. I spent a lot of time imagining what that potential moment would feel like: the moment of realization, followed by panic, followed by some sort of painful, complicated reckoning. When that moment actually happened, it wasn't what I thought it would be at all. Everyone says it's the most difficult decision a woman will ever make. For me, it wasn't a decision at all. The moment I realized I was pregnant was the same moment in which I realized I'd be having an abortion. And that just felt . . . strangely fine. I wasn't really scared of anything. I knew where to go. And I knew that I could tell the people close to me and that they were going to support me. I live in Seattle. It's one of the most liberal, secular cities in the country, and the people close to me reflect that. My abortion never really felt like it needed to be a secret, because I wasn't nervous about anyone's judgment. And that's the only reason things are secret, right?

The day I found out I was pregnant, I wrote a BCC'd email to a dozen or so friends and family members. Subject line: "Guess What?"

Hello! I am pregnant.

I went on to explain the particulars of the situation, including when and where I'd be having my abortion, and closed with this:

I feel powerful and resolved and I don't expect any serious confusion to sneak up on me about this, not that I'm completely ruling it out. I just don't want a baby right now so I'm not going to have one. I love you and wanted you to know that this is happening, and that I'm okay. You can check in with me anytime but don't feel obligated. I've got everything I need and sort of want to just lay low.

A week or so later, I had my abortion. The procedure itself was uneventful. I went home and curled up, relieved that I was no longer pregnant. For more about my abortion, see page 66.

A year or so later, Planned Parenthood was under attack. A group of anti-choice propagandists had released a series of videos that purported to show employees of Planned Parenthood discussing the sale of fetal tissue on the black market. The assertion was ludicrous but incredibly damaging. Republicans in Congress saw their opportunity to capitalize and launched an effort to strip Planned Parenthood of federal funding, to the tune of $450 million.

I was incensed. In part because I'd had my abortion at Planned Parenthood the previous year, the injustice of the whole situation felt strangely personal. At the time, I was tending bar and working my way through graduate school, and I was so fixated on the situation that I brought it up constantly. I generally didn't reference my own abortion in these conversations. And the angrier I became, the more that omission weighed on me. I felt like I was dancing around the very core of my conviction, even in conversations with people who were just as angry as I was, simply because most bartenders don't talk about their abortions while they mix drinks. This might seem like a good enough reason, but also, it's not.

I gradually started to mention my abortion in conversations with acquaintances and people I didn't know at all, and with friends I hadn't already told. And fairly often, the person I was talking to would tell me that they'd had an abortion too. Some of these people had been my friends for years, and it shocked us to realize that we'd never known this about each other. Gradually, over the course of the summer, my friends and I started to talk about the fact that we weren't talking about our abortions. I talked to Lindy. My friend Kimberly Morrison and I decided to start working on a zine. I met a writer named Lesley Hazleton who had been angry about this for decades, and Lesley and I started talking about recording a bunch of abortion stories and starting a YouTube channel.

The morning that the House of Representatives voted to defund Planned Parenthood, I couldn't stop thinking about the staff at my neighborhood clinic. I imagined them having hushed conversations in corners, hugging each other, working to keep their anxiety away from patients. I unraveled. In that moment I felt desperate to align myself with the women who had taken care of me, not because Planned Parenthood provides cancer screenings and birth control and pap smears, but because Planned Parenthood provides abortion, and they'd provided mine, and my abortion gave me the whole rest of my life. Without more than a few moments of deliberation, I gathered myself up and dumped my feelings into a status update on Facebook.

I hit "post" and left for class.

Amelia Bonow
September 19 ·

Hi guys! Like a year ago I had an abortion at the Planned Parenthood on Madison Ave, and I remember this experience with a nearly inexpressible level of gratitude. I would tell you all about the exceptional level of care I received from every single woman at the clinic on that day, but I'm going to wait because I wrote something which I will share down the road in conjunction with a project that Kimberly Morrison and I are working on. I am telling you this today because the narrative of those working to defund Planned Parenthood relies on the assumption that abortion is still something to be whispered about. Plenty of people still believe that on some level-- if you are a good woman-- abortion is a choice which should accompanied by some level of sadness, shame or regret. But you know what? I have a good heart and having an abortion made me happy in a totally unqualified way. Why wouldn't I be happy that I was not forced to become a mother?

I was a little bit giddy, imagining my uncles and former teachers and bosses stumbling upon my post and being pushed into what I felt might be a constructive place of discomfort. I texted Lindy a screenshot of my post.

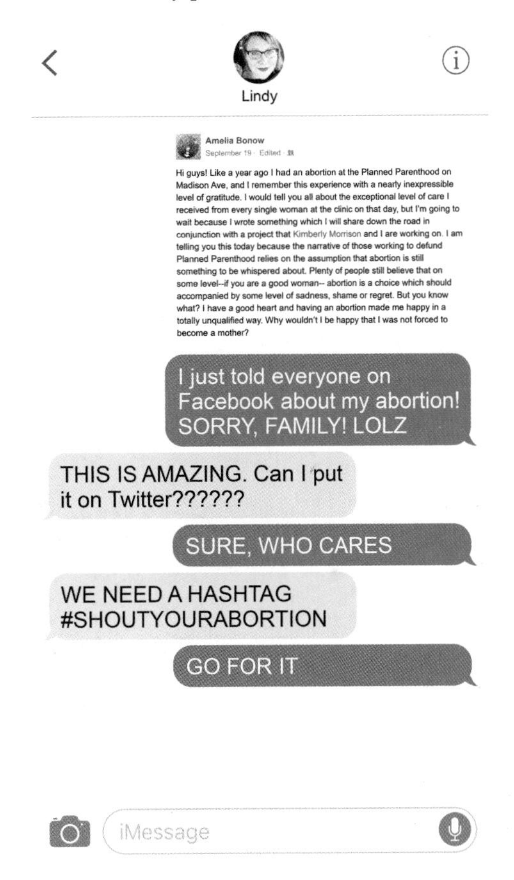

I got on the bus. I looked out the window for exactly one block, and then I checked my phone. A couple of my Facebook friends had already shared my status update along with a sentence or two about their own abortions. Lindy was texting me in all caps. I felt a jolt. And honestly, I think in that moment I knew exactly what was about to happen and that it was entirely out of my hands in the best possible way. ■

assumption that abortiuon is to be whispered
about." #ShoutYourAbortion
LOVE CELEBS BEAUTY FALL FASHION
SEP 23, 2015 @ 12:37 PM
10 #ShoutYourAbortion Tweets That Will Change How We Talk About Abortion
"The campaign to defund Planned Parenthood "relies on the assumption that abortion is to be whispered about." #ShoutYourAbortion.
After writer Lindy West read a friend's story on Facebook about having an abortion several years ago and her feeling that abortion was still "something to be whispered about," West realized that she herself hadn't been speaking openly about her abortion and wanted to help other women do the same. She asked her friend's permission and tweeted the Facebook post with the hashtag #ShoutYourAbortion and many women quickly did just that. Here are 10 powerful ones.
By Lane Moore
226
Shares
1. "Honestly, my abortion at 20 was one of the first responsible, non-self-destructive, grown-ass choices I ever made. #ShoutYourAbortion"
Ijeoma Oluo Retweeted
Diana Dee @DianaDee16 · 21 Sep 2015
A friend terminated a pregnancy because her abusive boyfriend got her pregnant so that she would never leave him. #ShoutYourAbortion
2 14 14
Follow
I was 20, in school and my bc failed. I did not want a child. It was the right choice and I've never regretted it. #shoutyourabortion
3:28 AM - 21 Sep 2015
10 Retweets 47 Likes
7 10 47
"All the News That's Fit to Print"
Cecile Richards @CecileRichards · 54s
Thank you @thelindywest and @ameliabonow for getting this going! Fearless women right here. #ShoutYourAbortion
Lindy West @thelindywest
The campaign to defund PP "relies on the assumption that abortion is to be whispered about." #ShoutYourAbortion
narrative of those working to defund Planned
Parenthood relies on the assumption that abortion is
5 years ago I had an abortion. I was poor, on drugs, & in ar
marthastahl @marthastahl · 21 Se
My abortion was between the birth
Made me a better mama to both!
abcNEWS VIDEO LIVE SHOWS
Seattlish
Also, if you don't want to #shoutyourabortion that's cool too. Just don't stand in anyone else's way. #shoutyourabortion
TRENDING
#ShoutYourAbortion: Hashtag Surfaces After House Votes to Cut Planned Parenthood Funding
How the #ShoutYourAbortion Hashtag
nd Sparked a New Movement
ADITI ROY and AUDE SOICHET
Share
Brie Ripley
I stand with my sisters who terminated pregnancies #ShoutYourAbortion
11:49 AM - 24 Sep 2015
Montel Williams @Montel_Williams · 32m
It is hypocritical to oppose PP & abortion AND oppose $ for social progs needed to help raise unborn u seek to protect #ShoutYourAbortion
45 114
Clementine Fo
I've had 2 abortions. I don't have to justify or explain them to anybody. My life is more valuable than a potential life. #shoutyourabortion
8:18 PM - 20 Sep 2015
242 Retweets 1,001 Likes
Setsu U @KatanaPen · 21 Sep 2015
Two days ago. First time. Relieved, grateful, grieving. Sending all love to those facing this choice. Trust yourself. #ShoutYourAbortion
6 4 13
#SHOUTYOURABORTION
#SHOUTYOURABO
The Washington Post
Style
MONDAY, NOVEMBER 16, 2015 · WASHINGTONPOST.COM/STYLE
THE NEW YORK TIMES NATIONAL FRIDAY, OCTO
witter, Push to End Silence on Abortion Goes Viral, With Emotions Raw
#ShoutYourAbortion tells the stories of those who reject shame and stigma
'I didn't feel sad. I didn't feel angry. ... And I didn't look back.'
ESSAY
Empathy or ego in our postings on Paris?
BY MAURA JUDKIS
I've never wanted to have children, so I had an abortion. I'm thriving, without guilt, without shame, without apologies. #ShoutYourAbortion
ELLE FASHION BEAUTY
SEP 21, 2015 @ 6:47 PM
#SHOUTYOUR
WOMEN ARE
Because "the campaign to
about."
BY MATTIE KAHN
2.4k
BY CAITLIN GIBSON
Amelia Bonow, a co-founder of #ShoutYourAbortion, wrote a Facebook post about her abortion that went viral.
Al Jazeera America @ajam · 24 Sep 2015
Social media campaign '#ShoutYourAbortion' stirring up controversy. @ines_ferre reports
Amelia Bonow
Hi guys! Like a year ago I had an abortion at the Planned Parenthood on Madison Ave, and I remember this experience with a nearly inexpressible level of gratitude. I would tell you all about the exceptional level of care I received from every single woman at the clinic on that day, but I'm going to wait because I'm going to write something which i will share down the road in conjunction with a project that Kimberly Morrison and I are working on. I am telling you this today because the narrative of those working to defund Planned Parenthood relies on the assumption that abortion is still something to be whispered about. Plenty of people still believe that on some level--if you are a good woman-- abortion is a choice which should accompanied by some level of sadness, shame, or regret. But you know what? I have a
#SHOUTYOURABORTION
CAMPAIGN GOES VIRAL AND SPARKS CRITICISM
#ShoutYourAbortion
A new online campaign aims to end criticism against Planned Parenthood, but has itself been criticized for its message
4 16 27
Leah Torres, MD @LeahNTorres
Follow
My birth mother put me up for adoption. Her autonomy was respected.
I provide abortions b/c I respect that autonomy.
OPERA REVIEW
A seco
I was 1
an abor
for me
#Shout
4:33 PM - 21
West, created the hashtag #ShoutYourAbortion on a Twitter account. "A judgment; it's the opposite of a whisper, of silence," Ms. Bonow said.

#ShoutYourAbortion is transforming
productive rights conversation
The New York Times
National Edition
THE NEW YORKER
News Culture Books Business & Tech Humor Cartoons Magazine Video
N #SHOUTYOURABORTION TURN
SHTAG ACTIVISM INTO A MOVEMENT?
By Vauhini Vara November 10, 2015
On Halloween afternoon, Amelia Bonow brewed a pot of coffee in her Seattle apartment and waited. Earlier, she had sent an e-mail inviting women to sit at her kitchen
Using the hashtag #ShoutYourAbortion, Amelia Bonow is encouraging women to share their abortion narratives.
C4
THE WASHINGTON POST · MONDAY, NOVEMBER 16, 2015
Unashamed and ready to tell their abortion stories
Erin Benzakein @Ebenzakein · 21 Sep 2015
Because tweeting about my 2 abortions was a more stressful decision than having them. It's time to #ShoutYourAbortion
Roza
Thank you everyone who feel brave enough to share their abortion exp. & for those who are silent, you are brave too! #ShoutYourAbortion
Lindy West
@thelindywest
Like, I literally don't even know what a "frivolous" abortion would look like. Steering your own future is not frivolous. #ShoutYourAbortion
Ijeoma Oluo
@IjeomaOluo
Following
Abortion rights is not just a women's issue, it's a class issue and a race issue.
#ShoutYourAbortion
12:56 PM - 25 Sep 2015
238 Retweets 462 Likes
April Greene
My abortion changed the trajectory of my life in a profoundly positive way. #ShoutYourAbortion
'Save These L
Shiloh Allen @green_converse7 · 21 Sep 2015
was 20 had 6 month old twin babies and was in a physically and mentally abusive relationship #shoutyourabortion
Jack Qu'emi
@jackquemi
I was 20. Among other things, the dysphoria surrounding a pregnancy as a transperson would have been a lot to cope with. #ShoutYourAbortion
10:25 AM - Sep 21, 2015
374 119 people are talking about this
#ShoutYourAbortion Gets Angry Shouts Back
By TAMAR LEWIN
FREE EVERY WEDNESDAY
the Stranger
#SHOUTYOURABORTION
KELLY O ON WOMEN'S RIGHTS AND COOL MOMS P.15
Abortion Rights
@Abortion_Rights
My life
My health
My education
My choice
My future
My body
My rights.
#ShoutYourAbortion
2:31 PM - 24 Sep 2015
Juniper Brown Jr. @JuniperBrownJr · 21 Sep 2015
#ShoutYourAbortion Hooray! Hooray! NO ONE has the right to tell you what to do with your body! NO ONE. YOUR BODY AND YOUR CHOICE. Period.
CNN
Women embrace, criticize #ShoutYourAbortion
By Michael Pearson, CNN
Updated 8:06 PM ET, Tue September 29, 2015
KEEP ABORTION LEGAL
& LOVE HOROSCOPES
CULTURE POWER & POLITICS LINDY WEST ABORTION RIGHTS
TION: THE NEW WAY
NG ABOUT CHOICE
lies on the assumption that abortion is to be whispered
Leit Motif liked
Aura Bogado @aurabogado · 21 Sep 201
Replying to @aurabogado
Imagine if anyone who wanted a vasectomy had to get an escort to the clinic because of the stigma. Unimaginable. #ShoutYourAbortion
ELLE
#ShoutYourAbortion Creator Amelia Bonow Is Tired of Talking about "Reproductive Health"
"If we don't own our own stories, they will be told by the people who are trying to snuff us out."
ed to stop pro-life rhetoric
STOP TAXPAYER FUNDING FOR PLANNED PARENTHOOD
MTV news
current events
These Women Are Not Here For Your Abortion Stigma – Let Them Tell You Why
#ShoutYourAbortion is here to set the record straight.
by rae paoletta 9/21/2015
Despite abortion being legal for over 40 years, the past few weeks have proven that the
BBC
Amelia Bonow
The women 'shouting' their abortions
Kuri
@therealkuri
Had an abortion at 18, went on complete degrees & live a fulfilling life. It was right decision in my circumstances. #ShoutYourAbortion
4:24 AM - 21 Sep 2015
7 Retweets 28 Likes
NARAL Pro-Choice NC and 1 other liked
Steph Herold @StephHerold · 21 Sep 2015
Abortion speak outs are powerful, whether in person or virtual. Collective experience is impossible to deny. #ShoutYourAbortion
Log Lady @jessicaloeraaaa · 21 Sep 2015
#ShoutYourAbortion My mother had one, back before she met my dad. If it wasn't for that, I might not have existed.
#ShoutYourAbortion

CLOCKWISE FROM UPPER LEFT: ZINES MADE BY SHOUT YOUR ABORTION BROOKLYN, SYA'S FIRST BUTTON-MAKING PARTY AT SPECKLED AND DRAKE IN SEATTLE, BUTTON-MAKING PARTY AT 20/20 CYCLES IN SEATTLE, AMELIA BONOW AND KIMBERLY MORRISON RAFFLE OFF A BASS GUITAR AT A SYA BENEFIT SHOW AT CHOP SUEY IN DECEMBER 2015.

ABOVE: HOMEMADE FASHIONS AT SYA'S FIRST BUTTON-MAKING PARTY IN SEPTEMBER 2015.
BELOW: SYA FASHION SHOOT IN JANUARY 2016.

#SYA VOL. ONE

BRAT Records

SHOUTYOURABORTION.COM

SIDE A

CHILDBIRTH- "I only Fucked you as a joke"
BOYFRIENDS- "The Future is female"
SSNACKSS- "Love"
CMRTYZ- "Feeling good"
DETECTIVE AGENCY- "why do I Try"
PONYTIME- "Time tells me"
VERSING- "Early Spring"
WIMPS- "Brew dawg time"

SIDE B

SHARKIE- "Post Marked"
DEEP CREEP- "Black balloon"
GREAT SPIDERS- "Bailey"
FIZZ COM- "Hospital (Part 2)"
CASUAL HEX- "Ego Sick"
MTNS with ARRINGTON de DIONYSO- "Dancing over old bones"
STEAL SHIT DO DRUGS- "Good agitations"
NIGHT BOSS- "Drop out of school, learn how to fuck"
MOMMY LONG LEGS- "Cat Callers"

SYA MIX-TAPE VOL.1 ARTWORK BY **BRITTANY KUSA**

#sya Vol 2

#SYA VOL. TWO

#SHOUTYOURABORTION.COM

SIDE A

mombutt - Jane's poem
Acid Tongue - Twisted
XCU - vagabond Life
Some suprises - Bones
Zen mother - Strange Feeling
Hoop - Bask in easy tone
Kelli Frances corrado - Rafael
mega bog - Black Rose

SIDE B

Clutch Douglass - This girl
Vatz - Drag
Scott Yoder - Ribbon of Hate
Lilac - Secrets
#tits - Bewbs (Diogenes Remix)
Vox Mod ft. Irene Barbaric - Flight of Fancy
Sashay - B-Squad
Beverly crusher - Golden Sceptre
Acapulco Lips - So Long

xoKS

SYA MIX-TAPE VOL. 2 ARTWORK BY **KERI SCHERBRING**

SYA BENEFIT SHOW POSTER BY **BRITTANY KUSA**

A #SHOUTYOURABORTION FUNDRAISER
A CELEBRATION OF
BODIES, CHOICES, STORIES
PRO-CHOICE! PRO-PARTY!
DJs
RAFFLES
JAN 15
7PM - 12
GMAN
TAVERN
3740
N CLARK
FEATURING
CARRIEANNE MYERS XELA DEL-CAMPO
MADISON MOORE MATT CIARLEGLIO

ABOVE: SUICIDE SQUEEZE DJ NIGHT POSTER BY **ANDREW LAMB**
LEFT: SYA FUNDRAISER POSTER BY **KATI MURPHY**

S H O U T S

our stories are ours to tell

ANGELA GARBES

When I try to recall details, they are frustratingly blurry: a ride up and down in a stainless-steel elevator, beige industrial carpeting, walls the color of cold oatmeal. Perversely, I remember reading an *Us Weekly* most of all.

I chose the clinic—the only one I ever considered—because a few years before I'd gone out to a bar with a friend who'd introduced me to her best friend. At some point, I asked this woman what she did for a living. "I help women get abortions," she said, beaming. "I love my work."

That I remember so little has been hard for me to accept. Ten years later, it still feels like a wobbly dream. It's not because the day was difficult or emotionally overwhelming. I suspect it has more to do with the combination of anti-anxiety and pain medications I was given. In the days after, I felt a tremendous sense of loss—not for the embryo, but for the physical sensation and memory of something that was important to me. For a long time, it struck me as wrong that my boyfriend, who held my hand through the procedure and is now the father of my children, holds more details of my abortion in his brain than I do.

It took years—five different jobs, a marriage, achieving financial stability in my career as a writer, giving birth to a child—before I could tell this story. Before I could tell my parents, the people who love me most in the world, safely and without damaging our relationship. And even then, it was out of necessity, an unavoidable truth. I consider it a privilege to be able to tell this story at all.

My parents are immigrants from the Philippines, a devoutly Catholic country. Abortion is illegal there and, for many years, birth control was too because "God will always provide." They've proven to be remarkably adaptable in their adopted country, including always supporting the girl who defied all their expectations of who their little girl would be. The high schooler who, when our church handed out bumper stickers saying "Life: What a Beautiful Choice," cut hers up and affixed it to the bumper of the old Volkswagen (purchased by her parents) to deliver a new message: "What a Beautiful Life."

HOW MANY STORIES DO THE PEOPLE WHO CARE FOR US HOLD?

I never told my mother and father because, while it is true that it's none of their business, it is also true that I wanted to protect them. Children who have seen their parents struggle to make sense of a culture, and repeatedly try their best to fit into that culture even as it denigrates and overlooks them, feel an extra sense of responsibility. As much as you need to rebel against them, when you watch them sacrifice comfort, home, being fully seen and understood—all for your benefit—you want to shelter them too.

Three years ago, I wrote an article about my experience with miscarriage that also revealed that I had an abortion. For me, life and loss, motherhood and independence, reproductive choice and lack of control over my body's workings are all tied in an inextricable embrace. The day before the article was published, I sat my mother down to tell her. I knew it wouldn't be easy, but I couldn't let her find out by reading it on the internet.

She began crying immediately.

"Well, it was your choice," she said. "But you have to know it goes against everything your father and I fundamentally believe in our hearts."

She went on to tell me about how she would have taken care of my baby, how my cousin in the Philippines, who is unable to have children, would gladly have taken my baby. How so many people would have wanted my baby.

My baby. I realized quickly there was nowhere for the conversation to go. The life she was concerned about was that of a weeks-old embryo. I was thinking of my own.

When my abortion was over, and I remember that it was over quickly, I lay there for a while, then got dressed and walked into the hallway. The woman I had met while out drinking years before was waiting outside the door for me in her scrubs. She gave me a hug, one I will never forget. She didn't say much and, in the 10 years and many social interactions that have followed, has never said a word about it. Her unfailing respect for my privacy moves me to this day.

How many stories do the people who care for us hold?

Abortion requires trust, placing yourself—vulnerable—in someone else's hands. For me, it meant turning my body and its memories over to others for safekeeping. For a lifetime. Now that I am a mother, I see that it was my first object lesson in the surrender that underlies my most important and rewarding relationships. There's another word for this submission: Love. ■

EVERYONE KNOWS I HAD AN ABORTION
EVERYONE KNOWS I HAD AN ABORTION
speak your truth.
i love u bro
ABORTION IS OK
abortion is normal
Abortion
GRITA
ABORTO
ABORTION IS NORMAL
#SHOUT
EVERYONE KNOWS I HAD AN ABORTION

LESLEY HAZLETON

I lived in Jerusalem from 1966 to 1979. The brief story is "I went for the summer and stayed for 13 years." The whole story? It hangs on an abortion.

I was as young and dumb as every 20-year-old has every right to be. Not that dumb though, since I was using a diaphragm thanks to the Marie Stopes Clinic, the one place in the whole of England at the time that thought unmarried women should be able to get contraception. And the diaphragm worked—until that first summer in Jerusalem, when it didn't. Not because of any fault in the device but because I hadn't put it in. Late in my menstrual cycle, I'd said, "Come on, it'll be fine." And three weeks later, I realized it wasn't.

The guy was good-looking, but that's about the best that could be said for him. We split up, leaving me a pregnant tourist in a foreign land, with a newly minted degree in psychology but no idea of where I wanted to go from there. The only thing I was sure of was that I was damned if I'd go back to England with my metaphorical tail between my legs. That and the certainty that since I could barely handle myself, no way could I handle a child.

But abortion was still illegal in Israel. And besides, I was dead broke.

I found my way to the Jerusalem branch of an aid organization for Brits—a single room with a single occupant. She took one look at me as I hovered miserably in the doorway, and before I could open my mouth she said, "You're pregnant, aren't you?" I nodded a mournful yes. "And you need an abortion?" Another mournful nod. "And you don't know where to go. And even if you did, you don't have any money?" I just kept nodding. "Sit down," she said, and picked up the phone. She made three calls. The first was for an appointment with a leading gynecologist who didn't believe in forcing women to have children. The second was to her HQ to get approval for a loan to pay his fee. And the third was to a publishing house to get me a job as a copyeditor so that I could pay back the loan. I walked out of her office breathing free again.

The procedure itself was a nonevent: a D&C under sedation, which was the standard procedure at the time. The doctor gave me a prescription for the pill, I languished on a sofa for the rest of the day, and, in the half century since, I've never had a single regret.

By the time I'd paid back the loan, I was in love again, so I stayed. I got my masters degree in psychology, became a journalist, and helped form the modern feminist movement in Israel—thus the newspaper photograph of me leading a pro-choice demo in front of Jerusalem's main department store. The sign I'm carrying says, "WOMEN, DEMAND THE RIGHT TO DECIDE." We did, and we got it. Abortion was legalized in Israel in 1977.

And the woman who made those phone calls? It turns out abortion can create lifelong bonds. Her family became my adopted family in Jerusalem. And even though I'd eventually move half the world away, first to New York and then to Seattle, we've been firm friends ever since. ■

LINDY WEST

When Life Gives You Lemons

I have no idea what prompted me to walk over to Walgreens and buy a pregnancy test. Maybe women really do have a spiritual phone to our magic triangles. I never thought I did, but that day I bought the thing, peed on it a little bit, and on my hand a lot, and these two pink lines appeared.

This was not at all what I was expecting and also was exactly what I was expecting. My boyfriend at the time was of the "I have grown accustomed to you because I have no one else" variety. We were careful, mostly, but sometimes people just fuck up. So I did what I always did when I needed a common, legal, routine medical procedure—I made an appointment to see my doctor. I was proud of my chill 'tude in her office. "So what's the game plan, doc?" I asked, popping the collar of my leather jacket like somebody who probably skateboarded there. "Why don't you go ahead and slip me that RU-486 prescriptsch and I'll just [moonwalks toward exam room door]."

As it turns out, THE DOCTOR IS NOT WHERE YOU GET AN ABORTION.

I went home and called a clinic (which had some nighttime soap name like "Avalon" or "Falcon Crest"), wobbling on the edge of hysteria. Not for all the reasons the fanatics would like you to think: not because I couldn't stop thinking about my "baby's" tiny fingernails, but because I was alone and it was hard. The woman on the phone told me they could fit me in the following week, and it would be $400 after insurance. I had just paid rent; I had about $100 in my bank account, and payday was in two weeks.

"Can you bill me?"

"No, we require full payment the day of the

procedure," she said, brusque but not unkind. I felt like a stripped wire. "But…I don't have that."

"We can push back the appointment if you need more time to get your funds together," she offered.

"But you don't understand. I can't be pregnant anymore. I'm not supposed to be pregnant." I sobbed so hard she went to get her boss.

The head of the clinic talked to me in a calm, competent voice—like an important businesswoman who is also your mom. "We never do this," she sighed. "But if you promise me you'll pay your bill—if you really promise—you can come in next week and we can bill you after the procedure."

I promised so hard. Yes, oh my god, yes. Thank you so much. Thank you.

I like to think the woman who ran the clinic would have done that for anyone—but I also wonder what made me sound like someone worth trusting. I certainly wasn't the neediest person calling her clinic. The fact is, I was getting that abortion no matter what. All I had to do was wait two weeks, or have a conversation I did not want to have with my supportive, liberal, well-to-do mother. Privilege means that it's easy for white women to do each other favors. Privilege means that those of us who need it the least often get the most help.

I don't remember much about the appointment itself. I went in, filled out stuff on a clipboard, and waited to be called. Before we got down to business, I had to talk to a counselor, I guess to make sure I wasn't just looking for one of those partybortions that the religious right is always getting their sackcloth in a bunch over. (Even though, by the way, those are legal too.) She asked me why I hadn't told my "partner," and I cried because he wasn't a partner at all.

I think there was a blood test and an ultrasound. The doctor told me my embryo was about three weeks old, like a tadpole. Then she gave me two pills in a cardboard billfold and told me to come back in two weeks. The accompanying pamphlet warned that, after I took the second pill, chunks "the size of lemons" might come out. LEMONS. Imagine if we, as a culture, actually talked frankly about abortion. Imagine if people seeking abortions didn't have to be blindsided by the possibility of blood lemons falling out of their vaginas via a pink flier. Imagine.

That night, after taking my first pill, as my tadpole detached from the uterine wall, I pulled a friend into a corner at a work event I couldn't miss and confessed that I'd had an abortion that day. "Did they tell you the thing about the lemons?" she asked. I nodded. "Don't worry," she whispered, hugging me tight. "There aren't going to be lemons."

The next day I lay in bed and ached. No lemons came out. It was like a bad period. The day after that, I felt a little better, and the day after that was almost normal. I wasn't pregnant anymore.

I sometimes hesitate to tell this story, not because I regret my abortion or buy into the narrative that pregnancy is god's punishment for disobedient women, but because it's easy for an explanation to sound like a justification. The truth is that I don't give a damn why anyone has an abortion. I believe unconditionally in the right of people with uteruses to decide what grows inside their bodies and feeds on their blood and reroutes their futures. There are no "good" abortions and "bad" abortions; there are only pregnant people who want them and pregnant people who don't, pregnant people who have access and support and pregnant people who face institutional roadblocks and lies.

For that reason, we simply must talk about it. The fact that abortion is still a taboo subject means that opponents of abortion get to define it however suits them best. They can cast those of us who have had abortions as callous monstrosities and seed fear in anyone who might need one by insisting that the procedure is always traumatic and painful. Every abortion story is as unique as the person who lives it. Some are traumatic, some are regretted, but plenty are like mine.

Paradoxically, one of the primary reasons I am so determined to tell my abortion story is that my abortion simply wasn't that interesting. If it weren't for mangled fetus photos, I would never think of my abortion at all. It was a medical procedure that made my life better, like the time I had oral surgery because my wisdom tooth went evil-dead and murdered the tooth next to it. It was a big deal, and it wasn't, but the procedure itself was the easiest part. Not being able to have one would have been the real trauma. ■

MANDY TRICHELL

With my baby brother on my hip and my four-year-old sister trailing behind me, I found the VHS tape of their favorite movie, *Who Framed Roger Rabbit,* and popped it into the VCR. It was the summer of 1990. I was 14, and I was often alone with my young siblings like this. We lived in New Mexico, and my stepfather worked in Georgia. He and my mom were effectively separated, and he'd been gone long enough for her to have already gone through a few boyfriends. This latest guy was a few years younger than her. He and a handful of his friends became my mom's party posse, including Steve, who was only 18. Mom frequently left for days with these friends, leaving me in charge of my little sister and brother. Steve started staying behind to hang out with me, rather than partying with the rest of them. We fell in love.

Steve wasn't my first boyfriend, nor was I a virgin when we started sleeping together in his bed. It was a love wrought with a feeling of impermanence that we pretended not to notice. He was a runaway from Lubbock, Texas, whose life seemed adventurous. Steve had no obligations, and he had a car. When he had a few dollars, he would take my little siblings and me to McDonald's. They'd play while we made plans to run away to California, because it was the furthest from anything either of us had ever known.

THERE WAS NOTHING ON THE SCREEN THAT RESEMBLED A BABY. IT LOOKED LIKE THE EYE OF A STORM.

About a month into Steve and I playing house, my stepfather came back. The babies were watching cartoons while Steve and I napped on the couch when my stepfather walked in with a shotgun. He nestled the end of the barrel firmly into the flesh between Steve's eyebrows and told him to leave. He was a rough-looking man, so big that he was ironically nicknamed Shorty. Six foot two, enormous belly, sticks for legs, dip in his lip. He'd been beating me and my brother Ian (who'd recently been sent to Louisiana to live with our dad) since we were six and three. He molested me when I was nine. He'd been reported to CPS, only to pack us up and move us to another state overnight. "I hate you," I screamed at him repeatedly, tears hot on my face. Shorty lowered the gun to his side and laughed. He said to the babies, "Come give Daddy a hug." He looked at me and said, "You done good taking care of them." Then he turned to Steve: "Go on, boy. Get outta here."

Shorty instructed me to stay put with the babies and left to look for Mom. I walked around the house in despair. I took care of the little ones. I didn't play with them. I yelled at them. I lay in what had been Steve's bed—a foldout mattress in the living room—and sobbed while they watched episodes of *The Smurfs*. The third morning after he left to look for her, Shorty walked through the front door with Mom. He had us packing everything up in a matter of minutes, and we were soon on our way to Augusta, Georgia.

On the road, I cried my broken heart out in the back seat. We stopped in Monroe, Louisiana, to visit family. I begged them to let me stay there with my dad, thinking that if I stayed a little closer to New Mexico, Steve might come for me and take me to California. It was summer, so Mom and Shorty let me stay, planning to return for me before the start of school.

I'd been at Dad's for about a week when I started having shooting pains in my abdomen and extreme nausea. After a couple of days of this with no fever and no sign of letting up, Dad took me to the ER. There was palpable tension in the car. I think we both suspected that I was pregnant.

I couldn't remember my last period. My breasts hurt. The way I felt reminded me of my mom's complaints when she was pregnant. The ER confirmed it.

I did not want to be a mother. My mother was 17 when I was born and forced by her father to marry the first man who showed interest in this young woman with two small children. I didn't want that life.

The days that followed involved phone calls to my mom, my Aunt Deedee, and my Mamaw (Mom's mom), who lived about 20 minutes from my dad. Mamaw came and picked me up. I spent a few days with her, waiting for my aunt to arrive and take me with her to Florence, Alabama.

Aunt Deedee is my mother's older sister. She was the first person in our family to finish high school and to get a college degree. She became the first female executive of a major construction corporation. I looked up to her and she looked out for me. She made it known that I could turn to her, and I often did. In my anguish and turmoil, Aunt Deedee talked to me about abortion, and she did so in a clinical way. She gave me brochures to read, told me about a woman she knew who'd had one, and pulled out the encyclopedia to give me info on *Roe v. Wade*. I began to feel a sense of hope.

I was with Aunt Deedee for a few weeks before Mom arrived. The first thing she said to me was, "You're gonna call that boy tomorrow and ask him to help pay for this." This would be the first time Steve and I had spoken since Shorty held a gun to his face. When I told him I was pregnant, there was a long silence before he simply said, "It's not mine." Tears welled up in my eyes, and through quiet sobs I said, "It is yours. Will you please help me pay for an abortion?" He insisted that my mom was making me lie to get money out of him. I felt like nothing, like I was the least significant thing in the world. Our story felt so Romeo and Juliet until that moment. It was my first experience being betrayed by a lover, and I've never felt so betrayed since.

My aunt made the arrangements and we traveled to Huntsville, Alabama, for the abortion. When we arrived, there were protesters. A man got into a yelling match with my aunt. He was so incensed that he followed her, which got him arrested for walking onto the property of the clinic. There was a woman who yelled at my mother, "You should be ashamed of yourself, bringing your child with you to this place!" Mom turned to her and said, "I'm not getting an abortion, *she* is, and if she were your 14-year-old daughter, you'd be doing the same goddamn thing." Maybe I should have felt embarrassed or angry with her, but I didn't. I was feeling seen and acknowledged by her, loved and taken care of.

The doctor who performed the procedure was male, old, and kind. I was only about six weeks along, so he said to me, "You can take a look at the ultrasound if you want to. It might make you feel better." I turned my head to see, and he was right. There was nothing on the screen that resembled a baby. It looked like the eye of a storm. "This'll be over before you know it, honey." Mom and Aunt Deedee each held one of my hands. I recall the sound of the extraction, wincing at the cramping, and Mom stroking my forehead the way mothers do when their children are sick. I slept hard in recovery, and more in the backseat of the car on the way back. From the front seat, my mother vacillated between being comforting and reprimanding. "It won't hurt for long, sweetie, just rest," she'd say, while reaching back and squeezing my hand; a moment later she'd turn and say, through narrowed eyes and a furrowed brow, "I sure hope you've learned your lesson." My aunt, ever my advocate, turned on the radio and distracted her with talk of what to have for dinner.

From that moment until my early 20s, I stayed on birth control. I became a mother at 22, and the decision to have my oldest daughter came from an empowered place. I had two more children and, long after they were born, I had two more abortions. As a struggling, divorced mother of three at the time, the freedom to choose abortion meant the quality of life that I was providing for my existing children could continue to improve. After my second abortion, I felt called to give back, so I began volunteering as an abortion escort. I also started talking with my own kids about sex and reproduction in the practical way that my aunt had with me. I took my teenage daughter to get on birth control when she asked for it. About a year ago, I began volunteering with Clinic Access Support Network, driving people to and from their abortions. My experiences have inspired me to be, for anyone who needs it, the person my aunt was for me so many years ago—an advocate, a facilitator, and a support. ■

This story was first presented at the live Oral Fixation storytelling show "Out from Under the Rug: True-Life Tales of Abortion" at the MATCH Theatre in Houston on April 19 and 20, 2018.

CLEMENTINE FORD

On a bruising winter day in the middle of 2016, I bent over the frame of a hospital bed and roared a baby into the world. I had been in labor for 18 hours, nine of them under the blessed relief of an epidural. I would spend the next two days feeling uncomfortably winded, my throat ravaged from the primal screams that had ripped through me as my son found his way toward breath. Over the last two years, he has become the most important person to me in the entire world.

The author Elizabeth Stone once wrote, "Making the decision to have a child is momentous. It is to decide forever to have your heart go walking around outside your body," and this has certainly been true for me. I would die for my son in an instant if I needed to. His suffering is my suffering, and I ache the more for it because I know I cannot prevent life from enacting its little cruelties against him.

You may think this a strange way to open a testimony for abortion, but you must understand one thing: my son, one of the great loves of my life, the person whose happiness determines the music that plays in my heart each day, my darling, would not be here today if it weren't for abortion. His story of life is inextricably linked to the story of my own life, and that includes the two pregnancy terminations I had when I was in my 20s.

My first unwanted pregnancy happened as a result of contraception failure. I had been using Implanon, but didn't like the effect it had on my body (namely, that contraception seemed futile because it killed any sex drive I had in the first place). My boyfriend at the time was about to go away for a month, so I booked an appointment to have it removed. We had sex the night before he left, and as he made his way to the airport the next day, I headed to the doctor's office. It only took a few minutes to take the small plastic rod out of my arm. I watched as the doctor threw it in the bin.

I didn't notice skipping my first period, but I noticed my second. I'd been feeling dizzy and vaguely nauseous for a few weeks, but I chalked it up to a lifestyle in which dinner was classified as a bottle of red wine, a bag of potato chips, and half a pack of cigarettes. Three home pregnancy tests later and it was official—I was fucked. My boyfriend had only been home for three or four weeks, so I assumed I was only that far along. Imagine my surprise when the doctor told me I was approaching the end of the first trimester! Turns out that sperm can live for up to three days inside you, and that removing a contraceptive rod makes you *instantly* fertile. Lucky me.

But actually, *lucky me* isn't too far from the truth. As an Australian I have access to universal health care, which includes financially subsidized abortions. Our access laws vary state by state, but they still remain significantly less oppressive than many of those we hear about across the pond. I was raised in a pro-choice household. (In fact, it was my parents who took me to the doctor who not only confirmed my pregnancy but also wrote me a referral to the local hospital.) At ten weeks pregnant, I would be given a surgical abortion under a general anesthetic, paid for by Medicare.

My mother came to the appointment with me. I imagine it was something she wished her own mother had done for her on the two occasions she needed it. (Oh yes, so many of us have been there.) Later, after we'd arrived home, my father made me a cup of sweet tea and gave me a selection of bath products from the Body Shop. "For when you can use them," he said. I sat outside nursing the hot liquid and, unshackled by the terror and burden of having unwanted cells rapidly duplicating inside me, I took a deep breath and examined my feelings.

Reader, *I was relieved as fuck.*

Despite the comprehensive support I'd had, the prospect of going through an abortion was still scary to me. Anti-choice rhetoric is fierce, and the pro-choice movement has ceded too much ground over the years in appealing to the view of abortion as a utilitarian moral choice. Until the launch of Shout Your Abortion arrived to challenge this rhetoric, it seemed like the only acceptable things to say about ending a pregnancy were self-flagellating rubbish like, "It was the hardest decision I've ever made," and, "I think about it every day." That might be true for some people, but the vast majority of people surveyed privately about their feelings exhibit the same response as me—sheer, blessed relief. I had approached my abortion knowing it was the only choice that made sense to me, but I assumed the aftermath would be characterized by shame, sadness, and regret. Yet they were nowhere to be found. Instead I felt strong. Powerful. In charge. And yes, fucking glad to have done it.

YOU ARE ALLOWED TO FEEL FREE. YOUR LIFE IS IMPORTANT TOO. YOUR STORY MATTERS.

I felt the same way six months later when I chose to end another pregnancy. The choice this time had been slightly more complicated, because my mother had just been diagnosed with terminal cancer. I had always known she would make an excellent grandmother, and I told myself this was a chance to give her a sliver of that experience before she died. But perhaps the truth was less altruistic. I was afraid of losing the person I had known from the very first second of the very first moment of my consciousness, and I thought that having a baby of my own might be a way to counter the grief that was rising up to meet me. Now that I've been through childbirth and early motherhood, I'm glad I chose sense over emotion. A child is too big a responsibility and a trial to be used as a means of avoiding loss.

It's rare to hear people talk about having multiple abortions. I suspect it happens far more often than people feel comfortable admitting, because we've all been conditioned to believe we should only talk about them if we show the appropriate amount of groveling remorse. One of the loudest criticisms of abortion is that we'll all rush out to use the procedure like a form of contraception. Frustratingly, pro-choice advocates often make the mistake of responding to this as if it's an accusation we must disprove. But here's a radical idea—*who cares if that's how people use abortion?*

Listen, we aren't born with a single token that's good for one abortion each until we've used it up and then *too bad, you have to become a parent now!* Abortion is a medical procedure that we use as part of reproductive health care. We are allowed to have as many of them as we like, and certainly as many of them as we need. It is nobody's business but our own how many abortions we choose to have in our lifetimes, and the only people we are obliged to even discuss it with are the people who are trained to provide them.

But it is also okay to use abortion as a form of contraception because abortion *is* a form of contraception. It's a form of contraception in that it prevents a pregnancy from going to term and resulting in a child. It doesn't have to be the only form of contraception that a person uses, but it is a fundamental option available to those of us who can become pregnant. It is the contraception we use when others fail, and we are legally entitled to use it that way. Abortion isn't something we have to prove we deserve by having the "right" kind of unwanted pregnancy. It's something we are entitled to regardless of the circumstances of our pregnancy, because the provision of safe, legal, and affordable reproductive health care is a human right.

If you are reading this and you have had an abortion or plan to have one, I want you to know that you are loved. You are supported. You are respected. You do not have to define or justify your choice to anyone. You're allowed to feel grief about it if that's what you feel, but you're also allowed to feel gratitude. You are allowed to feel elation. You are allowed to feel free. Your life is important too. Your story matters.

I look at my son every morning and marvel at the progress he's making on his journey to becoming an aware human. His existence is arbitrary and random, one possible combination out of a million possible combinations. Yet the flimsy foundation of his beginning makes him all the more perfect to me. He is the child I was waiting for. Unlike the what-if existences that anti-choice zealots tell me I should offer penance for, he is here in all his beautiful, tangible reality—his possibility made even more so because of the choices I made all those years ago.

Abortion is part of his story as much as it is mine. Abortion is what made his life possible, but my life too. Abortion is a story worth telling, and I will tell it until the day that I die. ■

ANONYMOUS

My boyfriend has stage IV melanoma. He is enrolled in a study for an experimental medication that targets the genes of the tumor cells. The long-term effects of the medication are unknown, and when he joined the study the coordinators said, "Don't get anyone pregnant." Not only does it affect your DNA in unknown ways, but it is unsafe.

I had a copper IUD—one of the most effective forms of birth control.

I was feeling ill and decided to take a pregnancy test. It was positive. With no symptoms, the IUD had displaced into my cervix and become ineffective. An abortion was the only option. Failed birth control, dangerous side effects, almost certain birth defects had the pregnancy continued, danger of removing an IUD during pregnancy, a terminally ill partner.... Abortion was not a decision I wanted to make, but I was glad that it was a safe and easy option for me in Washington State. I had the support of my partner, family, and friends. I had the procedure at a Planned Parenthood and was treated with respect and dignity. It was painless, and they were able to place a new IUD (a Mirena) while I was there.

I will not be shamed by this. It was the right choice, the only choice, and my partner and I are stronger and closer because of it. ■

MIKI SODOS

It's been 14 years since my abortion. I was 27 years old, and it was a difficult time, to say the least. I'd spent the last year taking care of my mother as she battled cancer, and she died in my arms six days before I found out I was pregnant. I was doing drugs regularly, and the person who'd gotten me pregnant was my dealer. In the year leading up to my abortion, I'd spent my days taking care of my mother, taking her to the hospital for chemo, to all sorts of doctors' appointments, everything else that goes along with being a caretaker. I spent my nights bartending and trying to hide my habit.

I called my doctor the day after I found out I was pregnant. The very sweet nurse congratulated me, not knowing about the dread and panic I was feeling. My doctor referred me to my local abortion clinic and I had the procedure.

I honestly never really thought about my abortion much afterward because I knew that it was the best decision, but it *did* affect me. It was not an easy road. Ultimately the loss of my mother, along with my abortion, made me aware of my actions on a day-to-day basis in a way I hadn't been before. I can honestly say that without those two occurrences I don't think I'd be alive today. The path I was on was one of drugs and destruction. Instead, I chose to get healthy, and today I own two businesses in Seattle and am drug-free.

My abortion was the first empowering choice that I had made for myself in a very long time. I was drowning. I believe that my abortion was a major catalyst for me to get my life together.

I felt no remorse or guilt and had no second thoughts. I was lucky to be able to schedule my abortion easily and lucky that the majority of the cost was covered because I didn't make a lot of money. I was lucky that my father and sister picked me up and showed me nothing but love and support. The clinic and the staff were wonderful and the protesters outside were minimal. Many women are not as lucky. Our basic human reproductive rights are under attack, which is why I feel that it's necessary for us to be vocal and loud. We have all benefited from the work of previous generations of women, and I know the next generation will be able to say the same about ours.

MY ABORTION WAS THE FIRST EMPOWERING CHOICE THAT I HAD MADE FOR MYSELF IN A VERY LONG TIME.

In 2015, I was scrolling through my Facebook feed and I saw my buddy Amelia's #ShoutYourAbortion post. I was proud of her for posting something so private in order to help other women realize they were not alone, and I decided to write a post of my own. By the next morning #ShoutYourAbortion had gone viral. My story had hundreds of shares, and many other women had joined by adding their own stories and supporting the movement.

Soon afterward, a friend of mine came up to me at my bar and thanked me. She told me about her own abortion, telling me that she'd never spoken about it with anyone except the father. I realized at that moment that my shouting had helped her reach her own point of catharsis. In talking about this stuff, I've done a lot of healing—around my abortion and that entire period of my life. ■

ROSA

It was the early spring of 2005 in Ohio. My boyfriend and I had been together for almost a year when I discovered I was pregnant in a Planned Parenthood.

Like many 23-year-olds, I was irresponsible. In fact, just six months before I had failed out of my first year of college. I was never taught practical things while growing up, like how to balance a checkbook or manage time. No one ever told me about periods, sex, or birth control outside my fifth-grade health class. My own mother was a teenager when she became pregnant with me, with an abusive young man who would later molest me. Needless to say, I was not set up for success.

ADULTHOOD FELT LIKE I WAS BEING THROWN TO THE WOLVES.

Adulthood felt like I was being thrown to the wolves. It was a mix of alcohol, drugs, and late nights numbing years of abuse. I barely scraped by working at a record store and did not have any financial support from my family. I had no medical insurance. My menstrual cycles had always been irregular, and I wasn't even sure I could get pregnant. I had leukemia as a child and had been told that the chemotherapy could impact my reproductive system.

Sometimes I forgot to take my birth control pills. I hoped that one byproduct of my cancer (which I considered to be my second most major life tragedy, following being born to a teenager and a molester) was that I wouldn't get pregnant in spite of sometimes having unprotected sex and being inconsistent with birth control.

I had run out of pills and went to get a refill at Planned Parenthood. "Could you be pregnant?" they asked. They gave me a test and there was no doubt that I was pregnant. I was in shock. The clinician gave me a few pamphlets with my options. Based on my last menstrual cycle I was probably just five weeks pregnant, which meant I could have a nonsurgical abortion if I decided not to keep the pregnancy.

I called my boyfriend and told him we needed to talk. I'm certain he must have thought I was going to break up with him. Holding the pamphlets, head down, I told him I was pregnant, as if admitting defeat. My boyfriend, who would later become my husband and the father of my two children, looked completely caught off guard. "But you're on birth control?" He didn't know at the time that I occasionally forgot pills, or that I couldn't deal with being sober because my trauma and feelings of failure were too much to bear. He *did* know that this decision was entirely my own and said he'd support whatever I chose to do. I already felt pregnancy symptoms at that point—sore breasts, cramps, and overall discomfort. I wanted to decide immediately, because if I was not going to keep this pregnancy I didn't want to develop any lasting associations to the way I felt.

In one day, I went from thinking I was physically incapable of having children to needing to decide whether to keep a pregnancy. At this stage of my life, the reality of motherhood sounded like a nightmare. I could barely take care of myself. Why would I want to bring children into a world where kids get cancer, get molested by their fathers, and flunk out of college? It felt like an easy decision. I called the nearest abortion provider and made an appointment, which was actually two visits. My boyfriend accompanied me to both.

Spring in the Midwest can be unpredictable, sunshine one day and gray the next. The sky was gray the day of each of my appointments. We were not celebrating this; no one celebrates abortions. In fact, it felt like the only people who talked about abortion at all were the protesters who greeted me outside the clinic. My first visit included a vaginal ultrasound to determine gestational age, but not the kind from the movies. There were no smiles and happy couples holding hands. Only me and a nurse in a quiet room in Dayton, Ohio.

At the next appointment I was given RU-486, the abortion pill. There were actually two pills—one to stop the pregnancy and one to expel it from my uterus. I took one pill in the clinic and was given information about what to expect. I didn't feel anything as we left the clinic. I wanted to cry, because I imagined that is what happens when you get an abortion. I wanted to feel relief, because I imagined that is also what happens when you get an abortion. I just couldn't feel anything.

The next day I bled.

I bled heavily, as was to be expected. I bled so much that I had to set up a pallet on the floor outside the bathroom in the house I shared with a roommate. Two of my friends kept me company for a few hours, distracting me with music and movies. Once my boyfriend got off work, he joined me. Every time I went to the bathroom I wondered, "Is this it? Is this my... baby? Embryo? Barely fertilized zygote?" I wouldn't be able to see it anyway.

I wish I could say that my abortion served as an immediate turning point in my life, but it took several more years for me to begin processing my traumatic adolescence. Three years after my abortion, my boyfriend and I became pregnant for the second time. We were stable then, and I can't articulate how different things felt. We welcomed the pregnancy.

Sometimes I wonder what my abortion baby would be like and then wonder if that is even healthy to think. I don't regret having an abortion. I'm certain that if I'd kept the pregnancy, my life would not be what it is now. It would have undoubtedly become worse. I never felt able to openly discuss the abortion outside of a few close friendships, because I felt ashamed and stigmatized. I was used to feeling haunted by shameful, dark secrets. But as I become older, I become more comfortable in my skin and my choices. At this point, I refuse to feel ashamed of my abortion. It was a decision that allowed me control of my life and saved me from a life from poverty. I had an abortion and I am better for it, and I'm grateful to be a part of this movement and to share my truth. ■

QUEEN

My name is Queen and I am 53 years young. My life is simple, and it is filled with love and light. I own my triumphs and I own my past. I WILL SHOUT IT ALL FROM MY SOUL, PROUDLY!

I was asked to share my abortion story. It's a memory that others might find devastating, but I do not. Over the years I've learned my life experiences are defined by the way I process them.

When I was 18, I found myself backed into a corner. I'd gone away to college and my high-school sweetheart was at the same university. We were in love, or so it seemed at the time. We were both honor students and we'd study late at his place. We knew better, but "it happened." We'd never talked about safe sex. We never discussed the what-ifs, either. No matter how educated or intelligent you are, sometimes stuff happens.

Well, the next month, my cycle didn't come. I was terrified. "My daddy is gonna kill me," I thought. Not literally, but you get it. My father was old-school: he was rigid and didn't believe in abortion unless someone was raped. And that's not what had happened to me. But I hadn't been promiscuous, or fast, as they say. And I was smart! I made straight-A's in high school, I was on the dean's list for four years, and I'd eventually go on to get a master's degree. I'd stayed a virgin until college.

I was on a four-year scholarship, and I wanted to finish with a degree. I knew if Daddy found out, he would make me come home, get a job, and raise his grandchild—plus he'd be disappointed and ashamed of me. Adoption was never an option; my parents didn't believe in that. I had a plan for my life, and being forced to get married and be a parent wasn't part of my vision. So I decided to terminate.

I shared my plight with my mother and my bestie, who were both determined to stand by me no matter what I decided. Momma told me to find a clinic and let her know the details. My best friend and I found a Planned Parenthood, and my momma secretly sent me the money. My mother and I vowed never to speak of my decision again.

The counselor at Planned Parenthood spoke to me in depth about all my options. They had me watch a few videos and gave me a pamphlet, but my decision was made.

I'm not a religious person, but I am spiritual. And I don't believe that I am any less of a woman for making that choice many moons ago. My abortion was what was BEST for ME. I don't believe I am going to a place of fire and brimstone, nor do I believe that I should be ashamed. And I think the government should stay in their place. Planned Parenthood is awesome! They do more than abortion services—they offer HIV testing, pregnancy care, and so much more. No politician should be trying to close those doors, and nobody should be camping out in the parking lot harassing people who have chosen abortion. It is their right!

THEIR BODY. THEIR CHOICE. THEIR LIFE.

It saddens me to think what would happen without safe clinics. Back in the day, young women were forced into shady houses with no addresses and into dark hallways, resorting to abortions with rusty clothes hangers dug into their wombs. If we do not protect the right to choose, the outcome will be infection, death, and suicide.

I hope my story helps someone, and I am sending RAYS of LIGHT. It's always there! ■

THE LEGACY
LIVES ON!
ST. LOUIS

MEGAN RICE

When I was 15, I got a teensy bit pregnant. It was a couple weeks before finals my sophomore year of high school. I sat down with my 21-year-old boyfriend and we discussed our options. He brought up the fact he was making pretty good money on unemployment, and as long as my room was clean every Friday I'd get my $25 allowance from my parents, so we were like, "Let's have a baby!" Upon further review, I realized that was a little crazy and dipped over to my local Planned Parenthood for a quick abortion. It took me a long time to be comfortable enough to talk about this because I knew a lot of people would look at it as though I took a beautiful child out of the world, but I prefer to think of it like I brought an A in AP English into the world.

I'm a comic, and this is the joke I wrote about my abortion. There's a lot of truth in the bit, but some stuff has been omitted, and a few little white lies have been added in order to make it, well, a joke. True: I was 15 and secretly dating a 21-year-old. It *did* take me a long time to come to terms with my decision and to openly talk about it. Untrue: I didn't get an allowance. I didn't get into AP English. I never considered not having an abortion.

MY ABORTION IS ONE OF A FEW EXPERIENCES THAT I FEEL HAS DEEPLY IMPACTED MY LIFE AND THE PERSON I HAVE BECOME.

I knew I was pregnant before I got the actual medical confirmation. Women say this all the time: I just had a feeling. And I did; I just knew. It took two trips to my local clinic to come back with a positive pregnancy test. When I received my positive result, the young woman who delivered the news did so in perhaps the worst possible way to tell a 15-year-old she's pregnant.

"Wow. You're so young."

That was the first sentence I heard after being told I was potentially going to be responsible for another human life before I could even drive a car. I didn't even have my learner's permit. The woman began to go over my options. I stopped her and explained that I wanted an abortion. She said I could go home and think about it for a few days and come back. As far as I was concerned, there was nothing to think about. We scheduled my abortion for two days later, Saturday. It was almost time for finals, and I didn't want to miss school. The concept of ditching school for anything, even to have an abortion, was something I'd never entertained.

I left the clinic and went outside to my boyfriend who was waiting in his van. He was the exact type of guy you'd think would have a van and date a teenage girl. He did not handle the news well, but he did agree to drive me to the clinic and help me find a way to come up with the $350 needed for the procedure. How responsible! I called a few friends who I felt comfortable enough telling, and asked to borrow a little money. I had $100 saved up, and my boyfriend borrowed some money from his brother. With the financial aspect solved, I proceeded to go home and be a regular teenager for the next couple of days. My parents had no idea what was happening.

Saturday morning came and we headed to a different clinic 30 miles away, where the abortions were performed: an abortion clinic. I was nervous. I was worried there would be people protesting, and that I'd be reminded how young I was. None of that happened, but there were other things to be nervous about.

I don't really remember that day as a whole, but I have a few very strong flashes. I remember my boyfriend walking me into the clinic. He left and I went into the back alone. I remember sitting with my feet in the stirrups as the nurse performed a transvaginal ultrasound and told me I was six weeks along. I'd never asked how far along I was, and them telling me felt unnecessary and cruel. Writing that sentence now makes me angry. After that, in came the doctor and the anesthesiologist.

I woke up, groggy, in a different room. I was in recovery. There was a woman still asleep directly across from me, and the girl next to me was sitting up and drinking water. I had on what felt like a diaper. Once I was up, they gave me some water, made sure I was capable of walking, and opened what felt like a back door into an alley. My boyfriend was there and we got into the van. I was pretty out of it most of the drive home. He asked if I needed anything, and I said, "pineapple pizza." I had never had pineapple pizza before. Ever since that day, pineapple has been my favorite pizza topping.

I spent the next few hours in the back of the van in a residential neighborhood. Scream-crying. I mean movie-style, uncontrollable, hysterical crying. I'm not sure if I've ever cried like that before or since. At the time I thought it was because of pain, but in hindsight I'm not sure if there was any actual physical pain. I think I was just finally letting myself fully and emotionally take in everything I'd just gone through.

Did I do the right thing? Would I regret this for the rest of my life? Did I take a beautiful child out of the world? If I could give my younger self answers to those questions, I'd say: Yes, I did the right thing, for me. That isn't saying that a decision to not have an abortion would have been wrong, but I stand by my choice and am proud of who I was at 15 for being able to make such a difficult and mature decision. And no, I have never regretted my abortion. There were times I would wonder what would have been, what my life would have been like, how different the last 16 years would have turned out. But never for a second have I regretted my choice. As far as the last question: This isn't a theoretical argument about personhood. This is a personal story about my unique and singular experience of deciding something every single woman has the right to determine for herself, no matter the circumstance.

My abortion is one of a few experiences that I feel has deeply impacted my life and the person I have become. I'm grateful that I made the choice I did, for myself as a teenager, myself as a college student, myself as a comedian, myself as I am now, and myself as the future woman and mother I will someday become. ■

Goodtime Abortion

"...I love that donkey. Hell, I love everybody."
-James Tate

Mary got up late. She had been bound to an
enormous dream all night long and felt sore.
What was it? Anxiety nightmares, half starved
infants shrieking all around her, textbooks and
drums burning; ashes of a life abandoned. But
she wasn't afraid of that. It was a lovely spring
day. How 'bout a mimosa? Don't mind if I do.
Take a little walk to my doctor,
I love that doctor. Hell, I love everybody.

-Michael McKinney, 2015

THANK GOD
FOR ABORTION

VIVA RUIZ

I grew up Catholic and very much in love with Jesus Christ, so much so that I aspired to be a nun. Devotion has always come naturally to me. I understand now that the story of Jesus and unconditional love provided a safe place for me when I desperately needed one. I grew up in the hood, in the midst of the onslaught of crack cocaine. Not only were the streets a thing to navigate, but the home I was born into was as well. Children need refuge and will eventually find it somewhere, and in the beginning, for me, it was God.

In Catholic grade school I was shown anti-abortion films. A priest told me, "Sex is not something you do on the street corner like dogs." I remember that phrase distinctly because it lit up a part of my brain I hadn't been aware of before, and maybe not in the way he intended. There was clearly a mystery about the body that these people were viciously guarding.

I HAVE SEEN THE SHOCK OF AN IDEA BREAK A SPELL; IT CAN LEAD TO A CONVERSATION, WHICH CAN BE THE FIRST CRACK INTO A NEW PERSPECTIVE.

When I had my first abortion in the '90s, I was mostly surprised that it was not the trauma Catholic school promised. I did not suffer, inside or out. I wouldn't do it for fun, but I don't have teeth taken out for fun either (no shade to anybody who does). I was very much in love with the person who got me pregnant—a sweet and good person who transitioned a few years later. I remember her consoling me, saying, "The next time, you'll be having our baby." I did not need to be consoled. Another person during that procedure reassured me that I would still be able to have kids eventually, and I noted that there was a universal assumption around me that I wanted to someday have a child. I never really did. I'm open to it, but I've never been one of those people who absolutely knew they needed that experience.

I got pregnant a second time, years later, and if I was ever *not* going to keep a pregnancy, it was this one. A mess of abuse that mirrored the machismo of my upbringing was all up in that relationship, and I was really glad to be done with all of it. Regardless, I had some feelings about it; hormones crossed with romance are a powerful combination. I sincerely understand how abortion can feel heartbreaking, emotional, or traumatic. But it also needs to be said that a lot of us are not upset about our abortions, then, now, or ever. Because of this, there needs to be more space and permission for people to have all sorts of different experiences with abortions, especially since the topic is so thoroughly drenched with Christian and patriarchal propaganda that wants us to feel guilt, secrecy, and shame. I am completely unbothered by the health care I chose, and I wouldn't do anything differently. Abortion is normal. Autonomy is *joyful*. It is patriarchal programming that makes it seem anything but that.

The Christian Right are the obvious anti-abortion villains, but liberal hypocrisy is also incredibly counterproductive and damaging. A few years ago I was feeling so much rage about the frivolous new laws that were being invented to shut down clinics, and I kept ending up in conversations with cis white men—gay and straight—who sympathized with the Right's definitions of "life" and interest in my uterus, because people with uteruses were the ones "populating the earth." The horror dawned on me that the killer was inside of the house.

I started writing and sketching images, and speaking about abortion in a way that was beyond unapologetic. One design stood out: "THANK GOD

FOR ABORTION." I decided to print the message on T-shirts. At the time, I was demonstrating a lot against police brutality in #BlackLivesMatter protests, and the idea of sacred signage was fresh in my mind—as was the idea of being in public with a wearable message, something you didn't have to carry if you were running. While it's not necessarily an easy message to wear, and I don't recommend it everywhere—we have to stay safe and choose to agitate when and where we can—wearing it is an easy way to disrupt a space, and the status quo. (I hope we are all in agreement that the status quo is racist, femicidal, classist, ableist, and requires disruption.)

I think of TGFA as a tool that causes people on both sides to reveal themselves, like a special lamp used in hotel rooms to detect blood. I have seen the shock of an idea break a spell, like a sudden enlightenment or exorcism; it can lead to a conversation, which can be the first crack into a new perspective. I'm also encouraged to continue with this project every time people come up to me to hug me and talk about their experiences with abortion. I love and receive them and I can say I get it, I really get it, and I listen.

In the beginning, I didn't know I'd get to learn so much about this topic, but I now feel that part of my job is taking note and doing my best to speak to the things I can speak to, in an extremely imperfect way. For instance, there are places in the abortion conversation that could use more light shed on them. Where do trans and gender-nonconforming people fit into this? Abortion is important for entire communities, and communities are not made up of only binary-identified straight people.

I can see and feel the change happening in conversations. At the same time, the Right is more vicious than ever, but I am encouraged by every little change I've seen in the last three years. We cannot go back, and I am determined that we will win.

I also wrote a theme song for the project. It's a joyful thing to be in a cute look on a microphone singing, "Thank God for abortion!" and to have an entire audience chant back to you, "Legal, safe, and free." I use the word *God* because it encompasses all genders.

I am a person of faith and I know: If God is for us, who can be against us?

I walk joyfully, arm in arm with the rest of you, pushing in all the different ways you can push, toward our collective liberation. ■

THANK GOD
FOR ABORTION

ERIN

I have had four abortions. I didn't talk to anyone about them for years.

I remember when Amelia was asking people to contribute to a zine, before Shout Your Abortion became a thing. I was interested, but I definitely didn't want to shout about my abortions. I didn't want to talk about them at all. I had a lot of feelings about them, the main one being shame. I never felt ashamed in a moral sense—in fact I was pretty relieved—but I was ashamed in a societal sense. I sensed that one abortion was more or less acceptable, but four? That would be like announcing to the world that you were a total fuckup. And I didn't want to deal with any judgments or moral policing. I just wanted to keep my head down and survive.

ALL THOSE FEARS WERE IMAGINARY, AND THEY HAD TO GO.

As I watched SYA grow into a movement and as I began noticing the debilitating effects of secrecy in other areas of my life, my feelings began to change. I read more abortion stories and saw how fear and shame contributed to unnecessary pain for others. I began to want to talk about my abortions. I began to feel okay about them. I even thought that maybe it would make people feel better about their own abortions to know that at least they didn't have four. I wanted people who'd had abortions (many abortions, even!) to know that they deserved love and compassion. And I wanted love and compassion for myself too. I also realized that my fears of being judged a failure or a fuckup were not real reasons to stay quiet, especially when I had the ability and privilege to speak. All those fears were imaginary, and they had to go.

My abortions were neither terribly difficult nor easy. They were just a part of my life as a person who had sex, who had a working reproductive system, and whose life was sometimes complicated. (Sounds like a lot of us.) I thought about including details about my abortions in this story. I thought about talking about the circumstances surrounding them and the men who were involved. I thought about talking about how the life I have now would have been wildly different, if not impossible, without abortion access. I thought about talking about how I don't want to be a mother. I thought about talking about how much I love my nieces (so I must not be a "bad person" who hates children). But ultimately I don't think any of these things are relevant. They feel like justifications, and I don't believe justifications are necessary. I simply made the choice that I thought was best for me at the time. I feel pretty different today than I did when I had my abortions. Today I feel stable, capable, and clearheaded—yet if I had an accidental pregnancy today, I would likely still opt for abortion.

It's taken me a long time to talk about my own abortions with strength, grace, and honesty. It's taken me a long time to define for myself what Shout Your Abortion is. I know some people equate shouting with joy, and some find shouting about abortion to be abhorrent. I don't agree—and in any case I think shouting for joy is wonderful and we need more of it. To me, shouting feels more like, "Hey, world, this is what it's like to be alive! This is what happened!" And what happens in life is not simple. It's complex. It's both joyful and painful, maybe even at the same time.

I hope our society progresses to the point where talking about abortion is normal and accepted, and we can choose whether to be private about it. I don't think we can afford the luxury of privacy quite yet. We need to get rid of secrecy and shame first. Please give yourself love and compassion if you are going through an abortion for any reason. You deserve those things. And you are not alone. ■

AMY BRENNEMAN

It was the summer when I turned 21.

My boyfriend of three years and I were meeting up in Los Angeles, a city I'd never been to. I first visited a friend in the Bay Area and then hitched a ride down the Central Valley with friends of my friend.

My period was late. I sat in the backseat of the car, listening to the friends of my friend chat with each other in the front. I felt like a child looking out the window at the vast sky and fertile fields, a planet away from my quaint New England home. I felt a menstrual cramp—my heart leapt with relief! But no, I just had to pee. This happened over and over again in the five-hour trip down to LA.

MY ABORTION IS NOT SEQUESTERED IN A SHAME SILO, THE WAY MY MOTHER'S WAS.

There, I took a pregnancy test. John and I looked at each other and smiled with clarity. I was about to begin my junior year at Harvard. He lived in New York. We loved each other, we were dear friends, and our birth control hadn't worked. That was the whole story. We were both crystal clear and in deep agreement—it was not the right time for either one of us to become a parent.

We looked in the Yellow Pages for a doctor who performed abortions. We went to his office, cool and soothing, overlooking Sunset Boulevard. I remember his kindness, I remember my boyfriend's sweet support, and I remember being deeply validated for this choice I knew in my bones was correct. I remember feeling utterly connected to the little fledgling inside of me and communicating clearly with it: it's not the right time, little one. I'm not ready for you yet.

Afterward, we went to the hotel where John and his friend Ed had booked rooms. Enormous birds of paradise encircled the small pool where I sat in the sun and drank juice, peaceful. Inside, the television was on. A panel of white, male senators described the catastrophic psychological effects of abortion to bolster their position that *Roe v. Wade* be overturned. I laughed out loud. "What do they know?" I thought. I still think that.

Initially I felt ashamed of my lack of shame and confused by my lack of confusion. I never had a moment's doubt, one twinge of melancholy, or any remorse at all. That was my rock-bottom truth.

I didn't know if I'd tell my parents. I didn't know if I needed to.

I told my brother Andrew. He was kind and understanding. "You probably don't need to tell Mom and Dad about this," he suggested. I didn't disagree. Between Andrew and John, my experience had already been shared enough.

But when I saw my mother come up from the basement in our family home, holding an enormous basket of laundry, something vomited up out of me, wholly unplanned. "I had an abortion!" I blurted. She paused, choosing her next words, which were, "Is that why you went to California?" I was confused, not at all grasping her meaning.

Twenty years later, in 2004, I grasped them. It was only then that my mother told me of her own abortion. Mom was my age at a moment in history when young women had to travel, often far from their homes, to get illegal abortions. It was 1945, when she was a Radcliffe undergrad. America had just beaten the Nazis, and Cambridge was flooded with ecstatic, drunken servicemen. My mother fell into the arms of one, who disappeared in the light of day, leaving a fertilized egg in her womb. She went to the doctor—a woman—who was the only game in town.

My mother had lived with secret shame for decades. She sequestered her experience in a silo, hoping it would not bleed into her current successful life. She had handled it, I guess, but my heart cried at the lost connection between us. Why didn't she tell me about hers, 20 years prior, when I told her about mine?

Back in Connecticut in 1984, my mother nodded at my news. She said, "You probably don't need to tell your dad." I didn't disagree. Between Andrew and John and Mom, my experience had been shared enough. But still, it was odd. I was playacting a shame I truthfully did not possess.

In 2015, I was asked to be a part of the amicus brief in the Supreme Court case *Whole Woman's Health v. Hellerstedt*. The brief supported the statistic that 97 percent of women who have an abortions do not regret their decision, and in fact the opportunity to exercise agency over our bodies makes us healthier, happier, and more responsible mothers, should we decide to be. I was featured in a *New York Times* article about the brief. Before it was published, I realized I had never told my father about my abortion. Better do that before he reads about it in section B!

I was extremely close to my father, who died one year ago. He was a feminist to his core. Of all the people not to know, in some ways it was absurd that it was he. "Hey, Dad, I have something to tell you," I said to him as he flipped through yet another biography of Margaret Fuller. "You know I had abortion when I was 21, right? Well, I'm a part of a Supreme Court case on reproductive rights, and I wanted you to know before it hit the paper."

My dad didn't flinch. "That's wonderful, honey," he said, patting my knee.

After all that, it was like falling off a log.

I have now lived in Los Angeles for 25 years. The office of the doctor who performed my abortion is in the same medical building as my dermatologist. My abortion is not sequestered in a shame silo, the way my mother's was. It has been thoroughly integrated into my daily life; it is part of the story of who I am. In the years since that abortion, I have become a wife and a mother to two children, one with special needs. For me, having that abortion allowed me to make wise choices for myself and those I love. At the tender age of 21, society told me that I had a say in creating my life and that what I thought mattered.

The simple truth is this: if a sperm and egg come together when a child is desired, a human being is born. But if a sperm and egg come together when a woman knows in her bones that it is not the right time for her to be a mother, then perhaps what is born is her own confident agency over her life. ■

ABORTION IS NORMAL
EXIT 167
Mercer St
Seattle Center
LEFT 3/4 MILE
EXIT 166
Olive Way
RIGHT 1/4 MILE

MEGAN L. HARDING

Meditations on Abortion

Part I

I reach deep inside the warmth of my body to remove the barrier we use to keep things the way they have been, and it's missing. The familiar, translucent ring is gone. Can you please help me find it? Can you get a flashlight? He stretches his familiar, long fingers in me and returns with nothing.

Part II

My body is predictable; it swells, it warns, then it bleeds. But the blood is missing when I peer inside myself. Hours later, the contraceptive ring I've relied on for months is still missing. I'm on the street and I need to get inside, but I left my keys at the office. And then they aren't in the office, and so they're gone.

The next day is Friday and we work from my bed together, stopping frequently to hold one another. His lips fit mine and unlock me, unhinge me. I nonchalantly pee on a stick to show him I'm not afraid, and while we wait, I shower. I even let the hot water become hotter and I dwell there until I shouldn't. On the counter, on the stick, a second red line faintly appears. Can you please come here?

The internet—the space in which I work, in which I consume, in which I found love with him—brings me to message boards on mothering for expectant, or hoping-to-be-expectant mothers. I am part of a conversation where I am being told that a second faint line means that I'm pregnant, but I don't belong in the conversation because it's for people who want to mother. I use the internet to find a place that will remove me from this conversation because I am not a mother, and we go to that place.

We wait there for hours, and I am lost in a sea of women with bellies and other women with the same unfamiliar fear as me. There is a huge photo of a black woman from her neck to her toes, her belly bulging over her vagina. Her breasts are swollen with milk. A bad Katherine Heigl movie is playing, and when it's over, it plays again. He holds my hand and we respond to work emails from this strange place, doing the jobs we should have been at, feigning where we are and the illnesses we don't have.

My name is called, and it jerks me back to reality. Can he come with me? I enter alone, and the urine test and a sonogram come back negative. They take my blood and I wince. I have to wait 24 hours to know.

We go to Shake Shack and I eat an entire hamburger, which I haven't done in 10 years.

I pretend it isn't real for the night, as I celebrate my 23rd birthday with friends. Only my older friends show up.

The phone rings and I am in bed alone. The lady tells me to return in two weeks, because I'm pregnant. It's dark but it's only 1:00 p.m. I relay the news to him but he already knows.

Part III

I arrive on his doorstep. Since I moved two months ago, his doorstep is much closer, so we are much closer. I've never felt so close to anyone before, and I think that the only way we could get closer is by welcoming something we created into the world, or by saying goodbye to it.

We spend the day celebrating year 23 with my family. My aunt, her wife, my uncle, his husband, my mom, my sister, and her fiancée. We go to brunch together, and I wear a maroon dress—a nod to the period I never got. We call my mom later, the two of us on speakerphone as we walk home from a park that we do not frequent. We stop on the sidewalk and deliver the news. "I can relate," she says, and I feel so much better.

Part IV

I travel to San Francisco for work and spend time with my best friend, who was recently trained as an abortion doula. We smoke weed every day, she holds my swollen body, and we sleep soundly next to each other.

Three days after returning, I travel again for work, and I have never felt so exhausted or irritable. No one knows and no one cares why I'm not having fun.

Part V

He and I travel upstate to my mom's house. I never considered it "the country" growing up, mostly just a sleepy suburb. But in the autumn air it feels remote, far away, a sanctuary. I have never felt both further away and closer to confronting my reality.

I take the first pill.

We go to farms, we hike, we walk seven miles. I start to bleed as I'm walking the same exact walk I would travel with my other best friend when we were teenagers and we were both depressed. It was on those walks that we revealed we were both self-destructing, pulling up our sleeves to show each other the proof. Different types of blood. I bring him on this walk and it feels like I've come farther in my own life and farther with him than I ever expected of myself, had you asked me 10 years ago.

Part VI

I take the second pill, and he stays awake with me in the night through the discomfort and the blood. He passes me pads and looks into my eyes because he isn't afraid of this reality, of my past, or of me. The two of us share in the lack of a loss and smile about what we have.

Returning to the city, I thrust myself back into work, and it's too soon. I'm awake when it's dark and I return to him late. I'm still bleeding and I resent that it has to be a secret.

I arrive on his doorstep again. It's the only place in the denseness of buildings and bodies that I feel like I belong today. ■

Story originally appeared in SYA BK Vol. 3.

ABORTION
IS
NORMAL

KIRSTEN WEST SAVALI

As I looked around the dark bedroom, my eyes focused on nothing. I couldn't really see my husband's face as I told him that we were pregnant again, but I felt his body go still.

I gripped the sheets tighter as I felt my brain turn off my heart. "You know what we have to do," I said. "I've already called the abortion clinic, we can go Wednesday."

My husband, whom I'd met when I was 19 years old, turned to me and asked quietly, "Are you sure?" No, I wasn't sure. I just knew that we had three sons growing as fast as the pile of bills stuffed inside of my purse and in a drawer in the kitchen. The thought of growing big with another child, one who would maybe have our eldest son's face, our middle's son's smile, and our youngest son's hair—with eyes that would be a surprise as her fingers curled around my mine and they nursed for the first time—filled me with a joy so deep, I felt dizzy.

My mother died when I was 16 months old. As a young girl, I always said I wanted all boys—boys who would remind me of my father, my uncles, and my baby brothers whom I loved so much. But as my feminism evolved, I smiled as I imagined the conversations that I would have with my daughter about the beauty of black womanhood, the power in radicalism, and how to navigate the world free. I would be able to teach her things that no one had taught me—things I had to learn the hard way.

Of course, whether our new baby grew up to be a boy, girl, or gender-nonconforming, I would be in love, but it's always the dreaming that's beautiful, you know? The mystery of the stardust that would one day become a child. But we were a couple of years removed from poverty. It was time to rebuild our credit, create a savings plan and stick to it, spend more time together as a couple outside of our children, and spend more time with the children I already had. As I walked beside the security guard on the way into the clinic, a woman offered to buy my child. "Don't kill it," she said. "Jesus loves it and loves you too." "MURDERER," one sign read.

I walked in and sat among women years younger than me. I could see the fear in their eyes as they sat beside angry mothers or uncomfortable boyfriends, or alone. One young woman was in a wheelchair and disabled. I learned later that she had been raped by her caregiver and that that wasn't her first time there.

A white man droned on about adoption options. He had to do it, he told us. He had to let us know there was another way and offer the literature for us to read. By the time I entered the cold room for the procedure, I was numb. I just wanted to get back to my family. I do not regret my decision not to carry my pregnancy to term. I wish there had been another way. I wish we didn't live in a fucked-up capitalist society that makes it difficult to survive if you're not wealthy. I wish we lived in a world where black lives mattered and that it didn't feel like a fist was balled around my heart whenever my 13-year-old son is out and doesn't answer the phone.

I wish we had a health care system that valued black women's bodies so that I didn't have to worry about dying during childbirth or after. I could have died during my last pregnancy. I still remember bleeding through sheets and the nurse telling me to get up and walk so that I didn't develop blood clots. "You've come too far for these boys to lose you now," she told me as she helped me sit up in bed.

I wish I hadn't felt so guilty for not wanting to have another baby, but I made the decision that was right for me and for my family.

And I am so glad that I had the choice. ■

AIYANA ISABEL KNAUER

The first time I shared my abortion story with a friend, it was with my best friend from high school. We were always in some sort of delayed synchronicity with each other, my major life events happening a few months after hers, as though I were following her just a few steps behind. Our abortions were a continuation of that pattern. Because of her, I knew which clinic to look up, and to ask them for a student discount, and that it would feel like the worst menstrual cramps ever, and that the hormonal changes might make me depressed—that everything I was feeling was normal, and that it was totally okay that I never had second thoughts, and that maybe I should get an IUD like she did afterward. She showed me the ropes, as she had so many times before.

The first time I shared my story with a group, it was an accident and I was unprepared. It was the beginning of my senior year of college and I was in a printmaking critique with a dozen male peers and a male professor approaching 70 years old. The work I'd made represented my abortion story. My work wasn't great and I was not great at explaining it. In trying to do so, my story just spilled out—one long sentence that took me maybe 15 seconds to say. My voice shook with sobs, I coughed and choked on that sentence until I spat it out, and then I just kept crying. It was uncomfortable for everyone who was there. My takeaway from that humiliation was simple: I would figure out how to share my story on my terms, through trial and error. I would learn how to discuss something that was still raw. I would learn to control my own narrative.

The first time I shared my story with a journalist, it was in the apartment I moved into after college. It was an illegal loft that vaguely resembled the set of *Swiss Family Robinson*, which housed up to a dozen punks at a time, depending on the number of transient friends sleeping on our couches and floors. I honestly don't remember much about the interview, but the journalist took my photograph, and I was one of several people featured in the article, which was published by Reuters. That was that. A few years later, a friend texted me a screenshot of an article in *The Atlantic* titled "A New Study Says Abortion Doesn't Harm Mental Health," which was accompanied by that same photo of me. I didn't mind; it was kind of funny.

IT HAS LONG SINCE CEASED TO FEEL LIKE A BURDEN WITHIN A CONVERSATION—IF ANYTHING, MY OPENNESS HAS SERVED AS AN INVITATION.

The first time I shared my story with a crowd of strangers was on January 22, 2016, which was the 43rd anniversary of *Roe v. Wade*. I'd met two women in a secret feminist Facebook group, and we'd responded to a public call for action from a woman named Amelia Bonow, who had cofounded a social media movement called #ShoutYourAbortion. SYA was calling for people in every city across America to intentionally talk about abortion on the anniversary of *Roe v. Wade*, publicly, privately, in whatever way worked for them. That day, the three of us held a fundraiser for the New York Abortion Access Fund that was also a release party for our first Shout Your Abortion Brooklyn zine. I wore a shirt I'd made that had a big banner on the front proclaiming: "I HAD AN ABORTION." There was music and food and drinks and a raffle, and way more people showed up than we expected. Ten or so people shared their abortion stories, we went through several boxes of tissues, and I got a little drunk to cope with my anxiety. I realized that it was the first time I had ever helped create a forum for other people to share their own stories about abortion, not just myself, and I went home feeling like we'd done something really beautiful and empowering.

In between and after these firsts, I've shared my story as an unremarkable few words in conversation among friends, as a crass joke here and there with the right people, and as a photocopied zine that's made its way around the world. It has long since ceased to feel like a burden within a conversation—if anything, my openness has served as an invitation for friends and acquaintances to share their stories with me or to ask me where they can get an abortion or if what they're feeling afterward is okay. It's an extended conversation that started with my best friend from high school, who never thought abortion was a big deal but who also acknowledged the complicated feelings that can accompany it, and it's a conversation I've been lucky enough to continue with many others. She helped me feel like my experience was normal. And it was. ■

#SHOUT
YOUR
ABORTION
Bikini Kill

SHOUT
YOUR

AMELIA BONOW

I am not going to explain the circumstances surrounding how and why I got pregnant, although the situation was strange. Often, women buffer the disclosure of their abortion with details that are meant to act as a justification for the procedure. Sometimes, when a woman gives you the back story, she is saying: "Please continue to respect me, even though I had the abortion I am about to tell you about, because it was not the bad kind of abortion and I am not the bad kind of woman."

Were you being careful or not? Did you let him come in you? Did you know he was going to? Why didn't you take the morning-after pill? Were you fucking more than one person? Do you know whose it was? Were you wasted? Is this your first abortion or your third? It does not matter. Pregnancy is what happens sometimes when people have sex, and an abortion is what happens when a woman becomes pregnant and does not wish to procreate. If she is lucky. If she, and whoever knocked her up, and her non-baby, and society at large, are fucking lucky. There are seven states with a single abortion clinic, but I had an abortion five blocks away from my apartment, because I am so lucky. I remember this experience with nothing but gratitude.

IT'S PERFECTLY REASONABLE TO FEEL HAPPY THAT YOU WERE NOT FORCED TO BECOME A MOTHER.

I took a pregnancy test in my friend Shannon's bathroom one morning after we had breakfast. It was an offhand choice to do it there; I certainly did not think I was pregnant. I just remembered the test was in my purse and I had to pee. I peed on it while Shannon did her morning routine on the other side of the door, stream of consciousness-style emptying her brain into the room and changing shoes five times. I sort of lost myself in her blather and forgot what I was doing and then I glanced down and saw the plus sign. I wandered out of the bathroom and pointed the stick at her. She looked at me hard, the way that people do when they are collecting data from another person's face in order to determine exactly what that person needs as quickly as possible. I set the test down on the coffee table and lit a cigarette. My phone lit up with a text from Michael, our other best friend who lives upstairs, and I told him to come down. He walked in, buoyant as always, and the two of us silently motioned to the test, which was lying on the coffee table and pointing at the empty space between me and Shannon like a do-over in a game of spin the bottle. He choked on some words and lurched his body toward both of us, his wide eyes darting between our two faces. We realized he didn't know whose test it was; I raised my hand like a teenager in detention and we all laughed.

I didn't feel bad or even necessarily that alarmed. The only thing I really felt was surprise. Then I felt a familiar wave of calm, which I've often felt following the shock of incomprehensible news. This wave is the promise of my own future resilience. It's sort of a mantra, although I have never invoked it deliberately; it's just where my mind goes when things are very bad. The wave says: you can do this, and after you do, you will take it with you, and it will be power. I'm generally pretty faithless, so this reaction is pleasantly incongruous with much of my nature.

Earlier that day, I told my boyfriend that I was going to steal a pregnancy test from Walgreens because my boobs seemed to be getting huge at the wrong time. I told him not to worry because pregnancy seemed wildly unlikely. He then made an excellent joke about how he was positive that he did not "shoot up the club," and asked me to text him after I took the test. I didn't want to tell him I was pregnant via text, so I texted him asking when he would be home from his errands and said I wanted to come over. He didn't ask if I had taken the test; he knew that I had.

I walked into his bedroom, which was dark except for some afternoon sun creeping through the blinds, and I remember the dust lazily dancing in the beams of light. He was in his bed, hiding most of his face. He watched me take off my shoes, and we each willed time to move slowly because we knew that once the silence ended nothing would ever be the same. He is not old, but in that moment he looked old, and he looked sad, and I felt sort of sad for the first time. I slid into bed, which is the best place for this sort of moment to unfold between two people, and I kissed him. I told him that I was pregnant even though I didn't need to. He sighed, and a few tears came out of his eyes. I had never seen that happen before. He held me really tight. Then he squeaked, "Are you mad at me?" which made me laugh because of course I was not mad at him, but how sweet and reasonable to ask; after all, he had knocked me up. Then he kissed me, and he looked at me, and he put his hands on my wrists and held me down and fucked me hard until I came, which was just what I needed to feel healthy and alive.

SHAME IS A THING OTHER PEOPLE *PUT ON YOU*; IT ISN'T EVEN YOURS.

Here is the part where I tell you about the actual procedure: I am not kidding when I say that I have had visits to the bank that were much more unpleasant than that particular morning at Planned Parenthood. The only thing that happens at the Madison Avenue Planned Parenthood on Saturdays is abortion. Every person you see in the clinic is having an abortion, or helping someone have an abortion. The moment I entered the clinic that morning, I felt myself lift and become stronger because of the women around me. I felt connected to every woman I saw, and I tried to make them know this with my eyes. I used my eyes to thank every nurse, and to tell every woman in the waiting room that I felt strong and I wanted her to feel strong too. As I sat in the waiting room, I felt clear and calm. The nurse called my name and smiled at me; I kissed my boyfriend, rose to my feet, and walked toward the end of a problem.

Before I entered the exam room, I sat down with a counselor. She was there to make sure that I was making the choice to end my pregnancy on my own volition, and that I felt informed and supported going into the procedure. She asked if I had questions. She held my eyes with hers, and asked me how I was feeling. I exploded into tears, because my gratitude felt inexpressible. I wanted to thank her and everyone in the clinic for believing in the importance of their work. For being proud of their work. Every woman in that clinic operated with a level of presence and care and intentionality that made me feel completely held. I didn't even need to be held by them, because I have never been indoctrinated to believe that abortion is anything other than a woman choosing not to default into a life that she doesn't want. Motherhood was not an option for me, so there was no choice to be made, and I felt certain that I would not feel guilt or sadness about the procedure after the fact. My conviction felt righteous in the most positive sense of the word. I tried to explain all of this. I tried to thank her enough. I told her I felt blessed. Exercising the right to control my own fertility, surrounded by strangers who felt like people I knew, made me feel like one of the luckiest women in the world. I am.

I don't remember the faces of the two women who were in the room when I had an abortion. This might be because I was high on pills. I got high because I like getting high, not because I was scared. If I was scared, that feeling was so inconsistent with the actual experience that it has been subsequently erased.

The procedure I had is commonly referred to as a Vacuum Aspiration, which tickles me because vacuuming is a thing you do in order to remove unwanted detritus from your life, and aspirations are hopes for your future, which can be destroyed by having children you don't want. It did not hurt.

It felt strange, in the same way that it feels strange when you are having your blood drawn and as the suction kicks in, you feel a quiet internal "pop" as something leaves that used to be inside of you. The whole thing was over in three minutes. I have had many more painful experiences at the dentist.

I do not want to invalidate the feelings of ambivalence, sadness, regret, or pain that some people feel after having their own abortions. Their emotions are real and belong to them, as my gratitude belongs to me. However, I ache for the people who feel ashamed of their abortions, because I think shame is a dangerous and counterproductive emotion. Shame is a thing other people *put on you*; it isn't even yours. I'm telling you my story plainly, proudly, flippantly even, because we've all been brainwashed to believe that the absence of negative emotions around having an abortion is the mark of an emotionally bankrupt person. It's not. I am a good person and my abortion made me happy. It's perfectly reasonable to feel happy that you were not forced to become a mother. ■

This article first appeared in Salon.com. An online version remains in the Salon archives. Reprinted with permission.

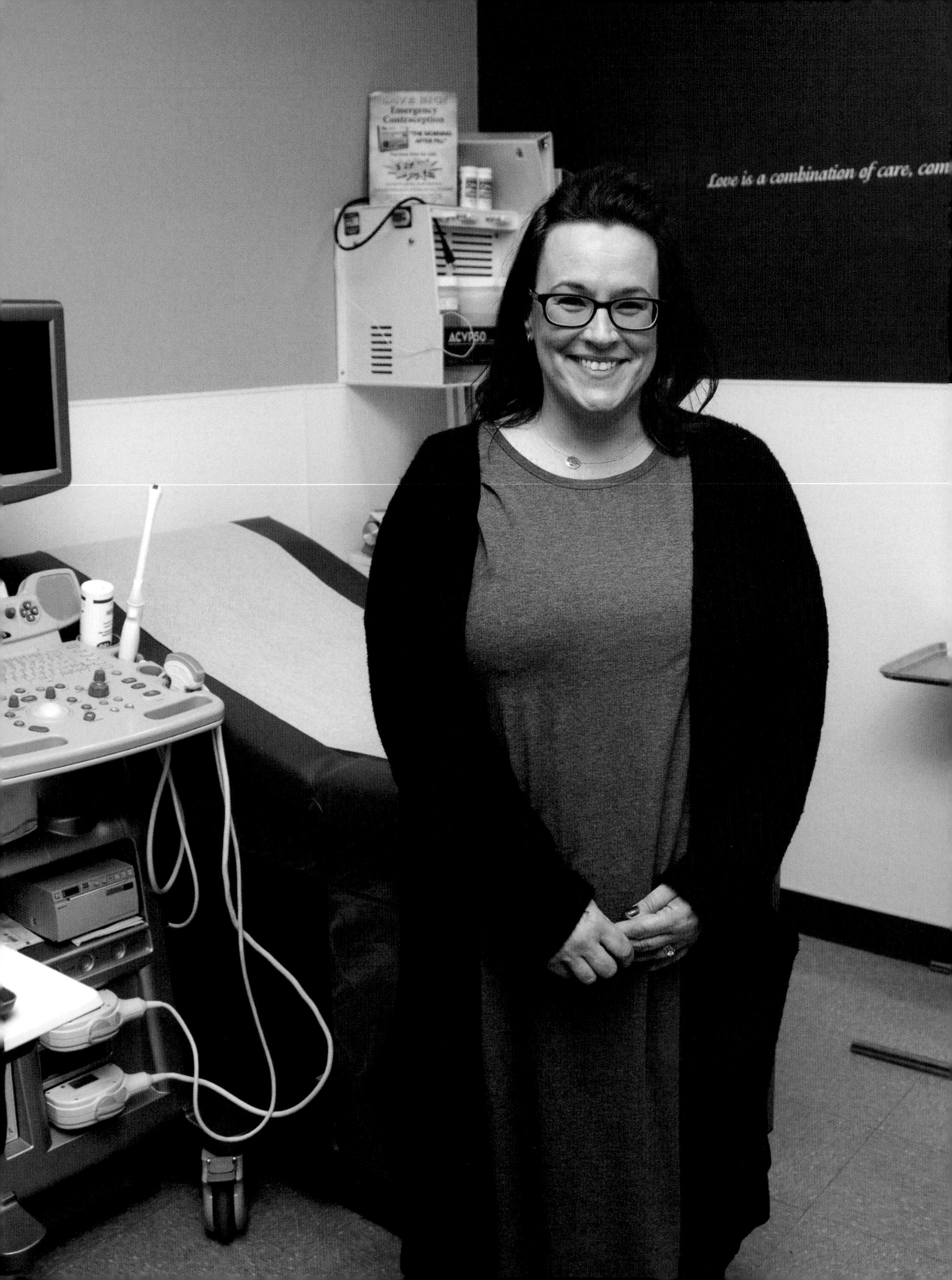
Emergency
Contraception
ACVP50
Love is a combination of care,

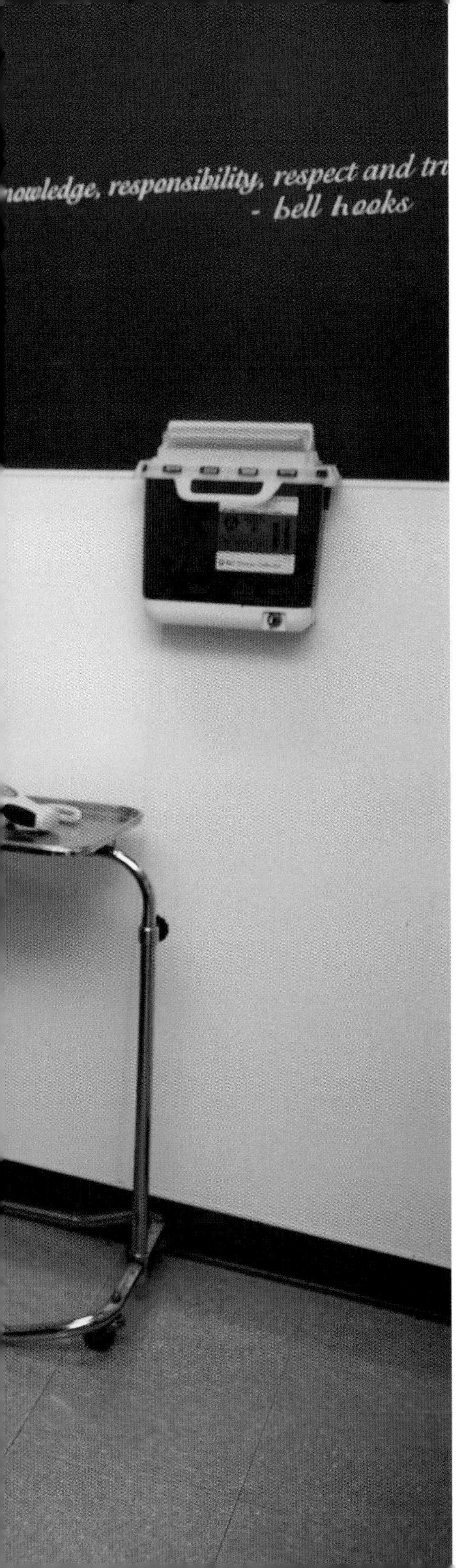

JENIFER GROVES

My mother didn't realize penises don't have actual bones in them until after she'd given birth to her second child. *Her second child.* She'd lived with my father for two whole years without any understanding of sex. On her wedding night, my grandmother told her that she'd soon be doing things with her husband that made her uncomfortable, but these things were okay because she was married now. My mother didn't have the tools to pass on reliable information to her children about sex, relationships, or consent; she's now in her 70s and she *still* doesn't have a basic understanding of how her own body works.

I was born the year *Roe v. Wade* passed, the fourth of five children. To my people, birth control was a sin and abortion was an abomination. Babies were a gift from God, even when the mother-to-be felt this gift was unwanted. Many women in my family would have preferred to be anything other than a mother, and their children would be viscerally aware of this their entire lives. Acknowledging that our mothers didn't want to be mothers is the only way we ever began to heal.

My grandmother died a few days before I was born. She was more than a decade younger than my grandfather, and she died at least 15 years before him. She'd given birth to 12 babies; not all of them survived. After her death, when her daughters spoke of her, they'd always say two things: how loving she was and how they remember that her bedsheets were always soaked in blood.

My aunt got pregnant in high school. We are big-boned gals, so she was able to hide the pregnancy. She gave birth, alone in her bedroom, to a baby who had the umbilical cord wrapped around her neck.

My Aunt Sharon would have been the best mom. She lost her uterus that night.

I knew as a child that sex would ruin me, even before I understood the mechanics of the act. I was confused by the idea that other people would try to prey on my body, but knew it was a certainty. As a result, my entire childhood revolved around trying to be perfect and keeping myself safe. With every fiber of my being, I felt that any sex that happened—whether by choice or through violence—would, in the end, be my fault. I didn't know what it was like not to live in fight-or-flight mode. I still don't. There was never enough food, warmth, love, or information. We scrambled. We clawed. We judged. We went to church. We put our heads down and confessed to things we had little control over. We prayed for our periods to come each time we made a "mistake."

I knew that my sister was having sex at a very young age, sometimes with family members. I told my parents. Nothing happened. I spent years trying not to be in that same position. When my sister became pregnant as a teenager, my parents disowned her. She ended up with four children before she could legally drink, and she was able to care for none of them.

I'm in my 40s and I'm raising my seventh child. Only one of these children was birthed by me. Each of these seven children has my whole heart. I've been pregnant as many times as the number of children I've cared for. A birth, demises, abortions, miscarriages ... these are my experiences. They've shaped me as a human. And they shape how I treat you as a human when you walk through the doors of the abortion clinic where I work.

I want my children to embrace their sexuality, love their bodies, and enjoy sex. I want the same for you. I believe people are inherently good and do the very best they can with what they were given. The threads which run through my life that I've described here may feel different than your own. Maybe there are some of the same threads in your own family, and these experiences aren't that different than yours. Maybe you can feel me anyway.

I am a very proud abortion care provider. ■

ABORTION

S. SURFACE

In November, during my first semester of graduate school, I learned I was seven weeks pregnant. University health insurance covered the costs of abortion, but instead of providing services at the university clinic, they sent me to the local Planned Parenthood. Its scheduling backlog meant I had to wait three weeks for an abortion. The appointment fell two days after my final presentation of the term was scheduled.

The atmosphere of an Ivy League graduate school of architecture is best characterized as "frenetic." I meant to protect the classmate with whom I'd become pregnant: *There is no reason that two of us should stress instead of one. We can discuss it after finals.* I made the appointment without asking him because if I waited any longer, the timing would have been even later. It did not occur to me that distributing responsibility and insisting on support were reasons enough to share. I tried to focus on work, to not think about it until it was time.

The miscarriage began around midnight, the day of my own final presentation. I told my professor that I was "ill" and asked if I could speak on the second day of presentations rather than the first. He refused my request. To reschedule would have been unfair to other students. I was not above the rules.

I could not explain my "illness." If I had, I believe the professor would have made exception. But school was not a place to be forthcoming about pregnancy. When a video circulated online featuring our dean explaining that women's architecture careers derail because they have children, all we did was sigh in exasperation. It was dismissed as curmudgeonly idiosyncrasy, rather than addressed as grievous bias that can be corrected through policy. In a place where professionalism was not misused to cover misogyny, I could have *told* my professor when I would present my work, rather than *requesting* permission to reschedule.

So, I delivered my presentation in a great deal of pain, slightly drunk, "suffering from food poisoning from a Boston cream donut" (the reason had to be funny) while blood clots seeped through my clothing. I believed in the quality of my work and was angry enough to address criticism without fear. I presented before that jury of elder white men while I knew that a dead thing was rotting inside of me, preemptively humiliated and disembodied past caring what they thought. For an hour, I gestured toward my drawings and models, mouthing technical terms while fixated on scraping my insides. My presentation went very well. Afterward, my professor caught me in passing and said, "I don't know how you did that." "That" meant our infamously harsh dean conferring his highest praise upon my work.

When I finally visited the clinic the next day, I was driven by a sympathetic neighbor and fellow architecture student, the only person I knew who owned a car. He mercifully asked no questions when I knocked on his door and requested a ride, *right now.* Of course, they had all of the tools and skills to perform an immediate D&C, the same procedure I would have had anyway. I got an abortion because the baby was already dead. There was no need to make me wait weeks or divert me to Planned Parenthood. Following the procedure, my neighbor retrieved me from the clinic, put me up on his sofa with red wine and cheerful videos of kittens, and left me alone to sleep. If he knew what happened, he never questioned me.

I imagine the medical obstacle course was designed to avoid controversy. Our health insurance covered the cost of abortion, so abortion advocates are satisfied. But elective abortion took place offsite, deflecting opponents away from the multibillion-dollar institution full of the world's most powerful people, and outsourcing the burden of their protests to a crowded, stressed nonprofit. Evil and clever.

Because I was made to wait weeks for the abortion, then an extra day during the miscarriage, I contracted a debilitating infection, then withdrew from a required class the following term to address my physical and mental health. Beyond the medical expenses, repeating the course added tens of thousands of dollars to my student debt burden. As a scholarship student, there was no provision for anything but a typical three-year course of study. This was all traceable to how I couldn't get a punctual abortion when I needed one.

Although I would have had an elective abortion, my own body beat me to it. I regret *not having* the choice, because the miscarriage raised so many questions. Perhaps poor sleep and diet, or exposure to spray paint, fiberglass, and laser-cutter fumes in the architectural model lab, made my body hostile to life. Maybe I was normal; miscarriage is the most common pregnancy outcome. Maybe my mind and body both knew the pregnancy was not viable. An elective abortion would have provided closure, because I would know exactly what happened.

Designers are taught to build stages for *others'* activities and lives. We do not learn to comport ourselves as citizens, but as experts outside communities. Simultaneously, we learn to be service providers. We abstract values into intellectual arguments, so they do not become personal. We are components of teams; we stand aside; we make ourselves small. We design abortion clinics, but we do not shout, "This work is important to us because we have had abortions." This work is important to me because I had an abortion. I bled through that presentation in front of those men, then got a copper IUD so I would not risk going through another unplanned pregnancy, then worked through my education, and then worked, and worked, and worked.

Nine years later, I got pregnant again.
In 2016 I learned the uterus can dissolve copper. Long before its twelve-year term was over, my IUD was stripped to its plastic skeleton. I did not want to be pregnant, but was fascinated that my body was *so* capable of nurturing life that it could eat through metal.

My new doctor left a copy of the *Shout Your Abortion* zine on her desk while I changed into my exam gown, so I trusted her before we met. She asked which options I'd like her to describe: surgical abortion, medicinal abortion, adoption, parenting. *"Tell me everything."* I knew the options but needed the ritual of hearing them aloud, insisting that someone spend time on me. This time, *"I'll talk to my partner. We'll decide together."*

I KNEW THE OPTIONS BUT NEEDED THE RITUAL OF HEARING THEM ALOUD, INSISTING THAT SOMEONE SPEND TIME ON ME.

Then the doctor asked me, "Do you want to see what I see on the ultrasound?" I did. I was grateful for time in the presence of my amphibious, aqueous child, sized and shaped like a tadpole, eye and heartbeat clearly visible. What I thought while looking at the screen was: *I see all of you. And all you can see is me, in a way I cannot see myself. I am your world, and I am not going to bring you into mine.*

I left the clinic to discuss options with my lover. We decided on medicinal abortion, and I scheduled the appointment. This time, it was swift. Under my doctor's supervision, I swallowed the first pill: mifepristone, to end the pregnancy. At home later that night, I took the second pill: misoprostol, to induce labor. Then the third pill: an opioid, to blunt the pangs of labor. I felt the moment it died. A few hours later, it loosened from my interior in an unceremonious toilet plop during one of many woozy sprints between sofa and bathroom. I wish I'd refused the opioid. If I could go back, I would experience the entirety of our pain and discomfort. Not to punish myself, but to be fully present while releasing that life from mine.

Despite grieving the pregnancy, I never wish I was raising that child. I am not confident that I did the right thing for my aging body—in the sense of *right* as in *correct,* not *right* as in *ethical.* The future can feel impossible when it brushes against the fact of our bodies doing what bodies do. We can become parents in our teens, and are capable of becoming grandparents in our thirties and forties. That this has become abnormal, disempowering, even *trashy,* is inhuman. Choice is not whole when one's livelihood can be gutted by bringing children into the world. If I were guaranteed to raise a child in a home of delight and abundance, rather than loneliness and hardship, would I have stayed pregnant? I might.

In my Japanese family, we recognize that a child is a life at the moment of conception, and also grant to parents what some in the West call the "right" to usher a soul back into to the spirit realm before it emerges into the earthly one. To exist in a spirituality of reincarnation is to be unbound to corporeal, let alone human, embodiment. In an ethos where the highest directive is "do no harm," abortion, in consideration of a whole family and community, can be a way to best follow that directive. We *know* that we harbor spirits in our bellies, and not clumps of inanimate, meaningless tissue. We grieve and remember aborted, miscarried, and stillborn children—our liminal "water babies," our *mizuko*—even when we know it is right to immediately make a child into an ancestor.

I wish I had chosen when to end my first pregnancy. I mourn the betrayals by the institution in which I'd grounded my life and future. I am glad I was able to end my second pregnancy at the right time. I regret that I didn't experience the full intensity of my second abortion. While these feelings are complicated and uneasy, my belief in the absolute right to bodily autonomy—the right to abortion—has never wavered. I do not always feel like shouting my abortions but I stand behind them, alongside others who have done or will do the same. Life, like abortion, is intricate and complex. Instead of justifying an impulse to simplify our options, this complexity allows us the full breadth of joy. ■

SENECA

I had an abortion 17 years ago, and there are only parts of it I can remember.

I was a poor college student living in a large Southern city, steaming along the way you do when you're popular and healthy and young. I remember it took me weeks to realize that the rape that nearly killed me had also resulted in me becoming pregnant. I'd lost so much control over my life and body at that point that I simply refused to connect the nausea, food cravings, swollen belly, and dysmenorrhea with pregnancy. I was still seething with rage about what had happened to me. I did not want to be pregnant. And I'd volunteered at abortion clinics before. Though it'd been years since they'd bombed the clinic in Atlanta, I knew about the potential of that kind of violence and wanted none of it. Instead I pretended I was fine, tried everything I could to bring on menstruation, and prayed. None of it worked.

I THINK ABOUT HOW MUCH MORE MEANINGFUL AND JOYOUS LIFE IS WHEN YOU'RE ABLE TO MAKE THE BEST DECISIONS YOU CAN FOR YOURSELF.

Eventually, finally, I could no longer deny what I was so desperate to have not be true. I tossed my 40th positive home pregnancy test into the trash and went to my primary care physician for an official diagnosis. I don't remember him confirming to me that I was pregnant, just the way he cheerfully asked when was the last time I'd had sex and spun the calendar wheel on a small rectangular card. I wanted to vomit, but instead I said aloud the exact date I had been beaten and raped. "About eight weeks." I remember him chirping that I'd be due that summer. I immediately started to cry. I told him I could absolutely not have a baby and that I wanted an abortion. I remember him telling me he couldn't help, walking out of the examination room, and slamming the door.

I don't remember how I got home. I also don't remember how I told my mom that I was pregnant and needed an abortion. I remember her never missing a beat, never doubting or ridiculing me. She just said okay, called her sister, and then called our insurance company. Next I must've looked up clinics online because I remember calling what seemed like a thousand fake clinics (aka "crisis pregnancy centers") before finally reaching a real clinic and talking to someone who could help me. Their voice was quiet and calm. They gave me a lot of information and I wrote it all carefully down. I finally stopped crying, and I remember having a tiny bit of hope because I had made the appointment.

I also remember having to wait nearly two weeks to get my abortion. I was terrified the entire time that someone somewhere would decide they knew better than me, and that I wouldn't be allowed to get an abortion after all. I was distracted briefly when unsupportive friends, and my rapist, learned I was pregnant and that I planned to terminate. I was able to meet the violence they directed toward me in an open and unflinching way. Being able to protect myself helped me focus my rage, regain my power, and strengthen my resolve. But mostly I went through the motions, pretended I was fine, and held my breath. Finally, the Friday came. I don't remember if the day was warm or cool. I do remember my mother driving me, walking up to a squat, nondescript building in a part of town I'd never been, and that the sun was impossibly bright.

I remember being buzzed into a beige, totally silent office and sitting among a half-dozen other people in a windowless waiting room. There were mostly women, some men; some seemed younger than me, but most looked older. No one said a word the entire time. We just waited. Finally, I was called in to speak with a counselor who asked me for medical details about myself, told me they were required to warn me about all the so-called health risks of abortion procedures, and asked me why I'd come to the abortion clinic that day. I remember saying that I was pregnant, that I'd come for an abortion, and then signing a small slip of paper that said the same.

Next, I was led into another room where a nurse explained I would have to have a vaginal ultrasound and asked me to undress. I remember her saying the procedure was required, ostensibly to determine the gestational age, but that really it just allowed lawmakers to add more pain to the process. She said it would be unpleasant but that it would be over soon.

She turned on the machine, inserted the wand, and a whoosh-whooshing sound filled the room. I remember the nurse asking me if I wanted to see the baby. I remember turning my face from the ceiling to the wall and telling her no. I reminded her that I didn't have a baby, that she was just looking at a clump of cells. I remember her then saying okay, removing the wand, turning off the machine, and quietly leaving the room.

I don't know how long I waited there alone. I only remember the doctor and an assistant coming in together. The doctor asked me again if I'd come there to have an abortion and, after I had confirmed this, again, explaining what they were about to do and how the process worked. Then all I recall were cannulas coming out, my cervix being dilated, the doctor's palm flattened against my abdomen, another machine being switched on, and another rhythmic whooshing sound. I don't remember how I got home. I just remember lying in my bed with a heating pad, falling asleep to the sounds of my mother busying herself cleaning my kitchen, and an overwhelming feeling of relief.

Honestly, I rarely ever think about my abortion. Most days I forget that I even had it. When I do remember, I mostly think about the particulars of my life that made me "lucky" and my abortion possible. In those moments, it's difficult for me not to connect the experiences 17 years ago to the ones I've had since being an abortion care worker and advocate, and parenting my 10-year-old son. I think about how much more meaningful and joyous life is when you're able to make the best decisions you can for yourself. And I remember: while I was furious about the needlessly punitive measures placed before me then, and how much angrier I am about the inhumane obstacles now in our paths, I am glad I had my abortion.

I am grateful. I've never had any regrets. ■

GRITA
TU ABORTO
KIRKY '16

DANA DAVENPORT

Ten years ago, I had an abortion. Five years ago was the first time I shared my experience with peers. Four years ago, I completed an art project based on the experience. Two years ago, I published an article on a major website detailing the effect my abortion has had on me both then and now. I thought I'd finally come to terms with what I'd been through and asserted for the world to hear that I had an abortion and I was not ashamed. Then, three months ago, I had a pregnancy scare. Faced with the possibility of a second abortion, I realized that my full reckoning was not complete.

I've gone through a few different stages since the abortion that have helped me work toward open dialogue. The very first stage was telling my parents I was pregnant and requesting help, more out of necessity than choice—I was a 14-year-old in Seoul, South Korea. The second stage was opening up to a group of peers after moving thousands of miles from home. It was then that I realized the power of trauma and how we are programmed to shield ourselves from it.

Early on, I found it difficult to recall specific moments from those weeks after I realized I was pregnant. I used to think I was trying to shield myself from the abortion experience itself, but looking back, I was trying to protect myself from being shamed. I doubted certain events and conversations leading up to and after the abortion. I've learned to state these foggy memories as facts. My mind wanted to forget, but I needed to remember and to say these statements out loud in order to work through them.

I had an abortion at age 14. I had an abortion and I do not regret it. I had an abortion and it does not encompass who I am.

Once I had affirmed my truth for myself, I wanted to turn that affirmation to face outward. The third stage in healing was to document it, which I did in the form of an art installation that recreated a sense of time and place. Feeling as though I had no control over my interpretation of memories encouraged me to record my experience the way that I recalled it six years later. The fourth stage was taking my feelings, my conclusions, and my journey and publishing them for the world to see—on the internet, with my photo, underlining the words "I am not ashamed."

BLACK WOMEN ARE VISIBLE IN SOCIETY AS CARETAKERS FOR WHITE CHILDREN, YET WE ARE VILIFIED AS UNFIT MOTHERS.

I have never felt ashamed, but rather I was shamed. I have never been embarrassed to tell my story, but I feared the backlash my family would endure from their close-knit community. I have never felt conflicted about the decision I made or the decision I would make today if I were to have an unplanned pregnancy. Yet three months ago, I had a pregnancy scare and feared the stigma I would face, even within the pro-choice liberal community, for having a second abortion. "My body, my choice"... until the second time around, that is. Still, I don't know whether my initial embarrassment was due to my own preconceived notions of what is and isn't acceptable or because I'd been made to feel that way by what society—even the liberal progressive pocket that I live in—deems acceptable.

I realized, feeling nervous and self-conscious about the prospect of a second abortion, that I had not yet completed my journey of reconciliation. I found myself looking outward in search of answers, just as I had 10 years ago. On the one hand, I know who I am. I am a 24-year-old black and Korean woman, artist, friend, lover, activist, community organizer, and much more. I'm a lot of things, but I am not my abortion.

Still, the experience has had an effect on the person I am today, and my trepidation about whether it would be acceptable to go through it again made me reflect on how far we still have to go as a society to ensure that people like me—human beings, women with fertile wombs, black women—all have the freedoms and options they need and deserve. It made me angry that the system in place has not been set up for folks like me. It is not set up for women—especially black women—to take authorship over their own bodies. Black women are visible in society as caretakers for white children, yet we are vilified as unfit mothers. We are more likely to die in childbirth, yet we lack access to abortion services. This facade is ingrained in our society, and it negatively influences how women of color see themselves, their worth, and their abilities.

My final stage is ongoing—it's continuing to talk about my abortion and freedom for all bodies to destigmatize, educate, and hopefully help others. ■

SONOGRAM

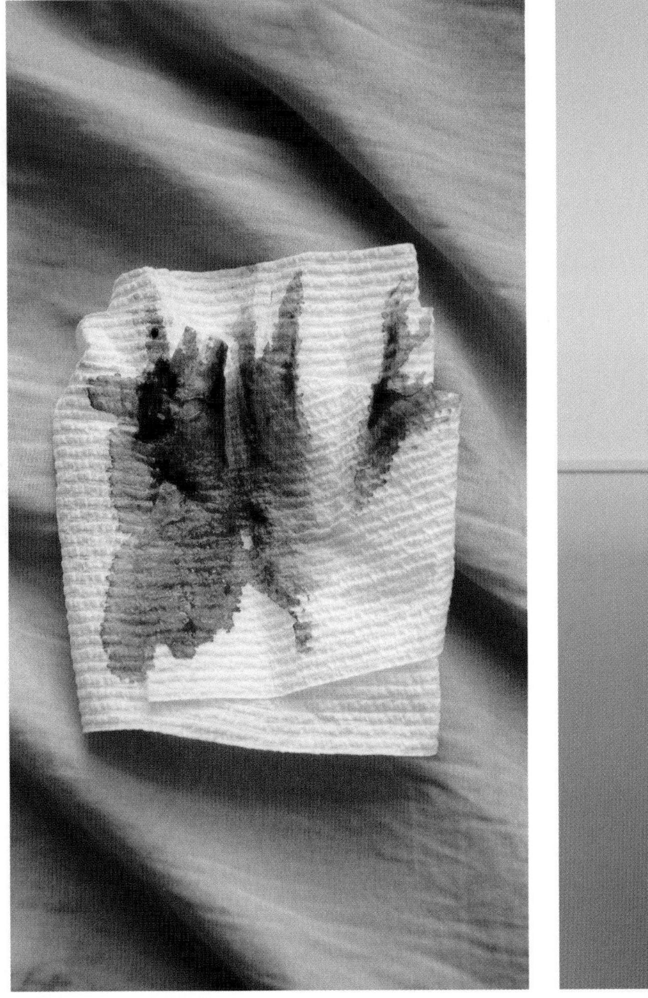

BLOOD

FOUR MONTHS (2013)

WENDY DAVIS

If you are reading this, you may be considering having an abortion, or perhaps you have already decided to have one. I am sharing my abortion story so you will know you are not alone.

Each year, many thousands of women decide to terminate pregnancies. Many do so because they just aren't ready to raise a child, because their career or school trajectory would be derailed, or because they already have children and they cannot bear the financial or emotional responsibility of having more. There are so many reasons—each unique to our own particular circumstances—that lead to the decision to terminate a pregnancy. And every one of those reasons is valid and should be respected.

YOU ARE THE ONLY PERSON WHO CAN DECIDE WHAT IS RIGHT FOR YOU.

In my case, I made a decision to terminate a very-much-wanted pregnancy after discovering that my much-hoped-for child was suffering from a serious and extremely debilitating brain abnormality known as Dandy-Walker syndrome.

You probably have heard that lawmakers have been seeking to ban post-20-week abortions. Mine was one of those. And it's one of the reasons that I stood for 13 hours on the floor of the Texas Senate filibustering an anti-abortion bill that lawmakers sought to pass there. Like so many of the things we tend to fight for, my position that day was born out of my own lived experiences.

When I discovered that I was pregnant for the fourth time, I was elated. I already had two healthy children, both girls, who would be much older than their new sibling. All of us—my husband, our two daughters, and I—looked forward with such happiness to taking care of this new baby together. When tests revealed that we would be welcoming yet another girl to the mix, our happiness was even greater.

We'd been through disappointment just a few years prior when another much-desired pregnancy turned out to be an ectopic one, meaning that the fertilized embryo was implanted in the fallopian tube rather than the uterus. This required surgery to remove the fallopian tube and, of course, to terminate the pregnancy.

I had only one fallopian tube left and would probably soon be aging out of the ability to have more children, so you can probably understand why we were all so happy about this new child. Our first indication that something might be wrong came after I had one of the routine blood tests that is given as part of prenatal care. Though everything seemed otherwise normal, there was one part of it that seemed a little "off." My doctor told me not to worry—we'd just keep an extra close eye on things. Then came a routine sonogram that showed a slight enlargement of the baby's head. Again, not enough to cause any real alarm, but definitely something to keep an eye on.

When I went back a few weeks later for another sonogram, which we all believed would be normal and would confirm our understanding that there wasn't anything to be concerned about, we received devastating news. This time, the sonogram revealed that not only was there increased abnormal enlargement of her head, but also that the two sides of the baby's brain had developed in isolation of each other, with no connection between the two—Dandy-Walker syndrome.

I will never forget how my doctor's hands began to shake as he guided the sonogram wand over my belly. Nor will I forget the look in his eyes as he handed me a box of Kleenex in anticipation of the reaction I would have when he shared the news that something was terribly wrong. Both he and I cried that day. But I still wasn't willing to accept that this was the reality we were confronting.

Instead, over the course of the next couple of weeks, my husband and I traveled to three other doctors to receive their opinions. Each only confirmed our doctor's initial diagnosis. Our much-anticipated baby had a debilitating abnormality. She likely wouldn't survive birth, and if she did, she would live a brief life of tremendous suffering. I couldn't bear the thought of either option.

And so, after coming to terms with what we were facing, my husband and I made the decision that we believed was in the best interests of our never-to-be-born child. We decided on termination. And we made the decision out of love—love for a baby we would never come to know. But we would do anything to spare her the suffering we knew she would otherwise face.

I couldn't sleep for days leading up to the procedure and truly did not sleep at all the night before. I talked to her throughout the night, letting her know how very much I loved her and how sad I was that I would never get to be her mom. The following morning, my husband and I went to our doctor's office, where we looked at her on the sonogram one last time and where I closed my eyes as the doctor inserted a needle through my belly to administer a medication that would stop her heart. Afterward, we walked together to the hospital where I had my third cesarean section, this time to deliver a baby who was never to be.

Fortunately, my doctor had provided us with some literature to read prior to making our final decision that included the stories of other couples who had faced a similar heart-wrenching choice. Some chose not to see the baby post-delivery. Others chose to do so. Each had their own personal reasons for choosing as they did, and it was helpful to consider their perspectives.

We made a decision to meet and name our baby. Tate Elise was brought to us by a compassionate nurse who had dressed her in a pink dress and booties. My husband and I each held her, shed endless tears, and said our goodbyes. Later, she was cremated and we held a brief memorial service for her in the backyard of our home.

This is a decision that I will never regret. And though I grieved deeply for a very long time and still grieve her loss to this day, I know that we made the best decision for Tate.

If you're reading this in the waiting room of a clinic, if you've decided to have an abortion or have had an abortion in the past: you are the only person who can decide what is right for you. Please know that you are loved, that you are not judged, and that there are sisters like me out here in the world who are holding your hand and have your back in this moment. Because, like the Planned Parenthood slogan, we care—no matter what. ■

Much love,
Wendy Davis,
former Texas state senator and
founder of Deeds Not Words

C
U

PRIMUS

AMY

I grew up in an affluent suburb of Houston, in an upper-middle-class household with two loving, supportive parents. I'm extremely aware of these privileges now, but I certainly wasn't during my formative years. I was a precocious kid, a trait exacerbated by puberty and my conviction that I was a big fish in a small pond that deserved better than Tex-ass.

When I started college at a prestigious liberal arts school in Southern California, my delusions of grandeur were quickly replaced by the reality that I wasn't particularly special when compared to my new peers; I was just a guppy in the ocean. Rather than cope in a healthy way, I decided to just get really good at partying and making questionable life choices. It was an effective way to mask my insecurity, until it wasn't.

I found out I was pregnant in the fall of my sophomore year, during a routine well-woman exam at the campus health center. I spoke to the guy I was dating at the time and didn't present options other than abortion, because at that stage of my life, what other options were there? He was supportive, paid for half, and took me to and from my appointments. There were no protesters outside the clinic that Wednesday (I think it was a Wednesday) morning, and the doctors and nurses were wonderfully kind and compassionate. I went home and tried to forget it ever happened.

Part of my facade of confidence and being blasé was maintaining an "It's whatever! I'm fine, I'm having fun!" attitude about most situations, but I felt that narrative wouldn't fly when speaking about an abortion. So I didn't tell anyone, flunked out of that college in a blaze of glory that would have made a dying star proud, and came back to Houston with my tail between my legs, utterly defeated. Then I started telling people. I figured that I already had the mark of failure on me, so why not? To my surprise, those people, including my parents, continued to love me. And then I met new people who loved me! Some had even had abortions of their own. It was around this time I started realizing how much my privilege was showing.

The state of reproductive rights in Texas was grim when I moved back in 2010, and, frankly, that hasn't changed. Our state legislature is nothing if not creative when it comes to restricting women's bodily autonomy. My friends have been subjected to mandatory ultrasounds during which the fetus's heartbeat is intentionally made audible, and in 2017 the Texas state legislature passed a law requiring abortion providers to bury or cremate fetal remains. The ultrasound and fetal cremation laws were devised to shame and traumatize women seeking abortions and to make abortion services prohibitively expensive for clinics to provide. But Texas pro-choice organizations have fought relentlessly and have won a couple of important, high-profile victories.

Shortly after passing, the cremation law was blocked in federal court, and House Bill 2, a set of regulations responsible for closing over half of Texas's clinics in the span of a couple of years, was overturned by the U.S. Supreme Court in 2016.

All but three of the remaining abortion clinics in the state are in major metropolitan areas, however, making it particularly difficult for women in rural areas to obtain abortions. My story isn't particularly interesting, and my current activism is limited in its scope. I didn't overcome gross obstacles to obtain my abortion, I had access to the resources I needed, and my friends and family supported me when I began speaking out. I know now that my abortion is nothing to be ashamed of or hide. I wanted to participate in this project to let other young women—who may feel a little broken, or less-than, or scared—know that they are far from alone in their experience.

We all have stories, and telling them reduces stigma surrounding an exceptionally common procedure. ■

BETTY

When I graduated high school in the mid-1950s, I needed to escape a difficult home situation, so I immediately married my high school boyfriend. After 15 years of working through college and professional school, and after having three much-wanted daughters, we divorced. I got custody of our children.

By 1970 I had married again and moved from my hometown in Tennessee to a Marine Corps base near Washington, DC. My new husband was a career Marine officer who had just returned from a second tour in Vietnam. He was also divorced and had been awarded custody of his five-year-old twin daughters. The seven of us lived in officer's quarters in a two-bedroom, third-floor walk-up apartment in an elegant building with steam heat and no air conditioning. A glassed-in porch became our bedroom, and the five girls shared the two large bedrooms.

MY FEELINGS TODAY ARE THE SAME AS THEY WERE OVER 50 YEARS AGO.

When I got pregnant during the first six months of our marriage, it was more than our family of seven could manage. The elation I had always felt during my past pregnancies was replaced by a feeling of panic that grew every day, knowing the extraordinary stress and problems a new baby would have brought to our new blended family. I had never considered the potential choices surrounding a pregnancy. It was before *Roe v. Wade*, and abortion was illegal in all states except in cases of danger to the mother or embryo, as evaluated by a psychiatrist or obstetrician. Furthermore, these exceptions applied only until the 20th gestational week.

I had not come to a decision and needed to talk to a professional counselor about my ambivalence. I expected that my husband would find out what was available under the military health care system or by word of mouth within the Corps scuttlebutt, but the weeks ticked away and nothing had been done. Assuming my husband would take care of this, I asked him about it daily. It was an emotional crisis for me, and I felt abandoned and scared.

Over the years since then, I've come to believe that the lack of shared responsibility during this early crisis foreshadowed similar spousal behavior. Our marriage would last 15 years but never truly recover.

Eventually, the urgency became clear to my husband. He gathered the necessary information and I went to a local psychiatrist. The doctor saw me for approximately 15 minutes and signed a paper, which I suppose declared that I was a danger to myself or others. He showed no interest in hearing of my ambivalence and in fact chuckled when I tried to introduce the subject. I got no relief from my anxiety.

The abortion experience itself was insignificant to me. The procedure was a dilation and curettage—a D&C—daytime surgery at a local hospital. Recovery involved a few days of rest and mild bleeding.

A few weeks later, a friend from our building knocked on our door. She told me that she'd heard what I'd done and was upset. She said that she loved children, had three of her own, and would have been happy to keep me from killing a baby by raising it herself. These hurtful remarks were a complete surprise—I had told no one—and cut deeper than I'd ever believed they could. My abortion story essentially ends there. Thinking back, it is marked by three things: the sadness I felt about my pregnancy coupled with an uncertainty of my options, my visit with the psychiatrist who did nothing to support me psychologically, and the pain I felt after being shamed by my neighbor when I was already deeply depressed.

The choice of abortion is not an easy one for many women. My feelings today are the same as they were over 50 years ago—it was a painful and difficult decision made more painful for me because of social condemnation and having the abortion in secret and without kindness and support from family and friends. But I have no regrets.

There is a very happy ending to my story: I have been most happily married now for over 32 years to a wonderful man whom I love, respect, and share interests with in travel, reading, music, politics, and movies. And now, at 82 years old, I have two adorable great-grandchildren! ■

Story appears on Tennessee Stories Project, https://tnstories.org

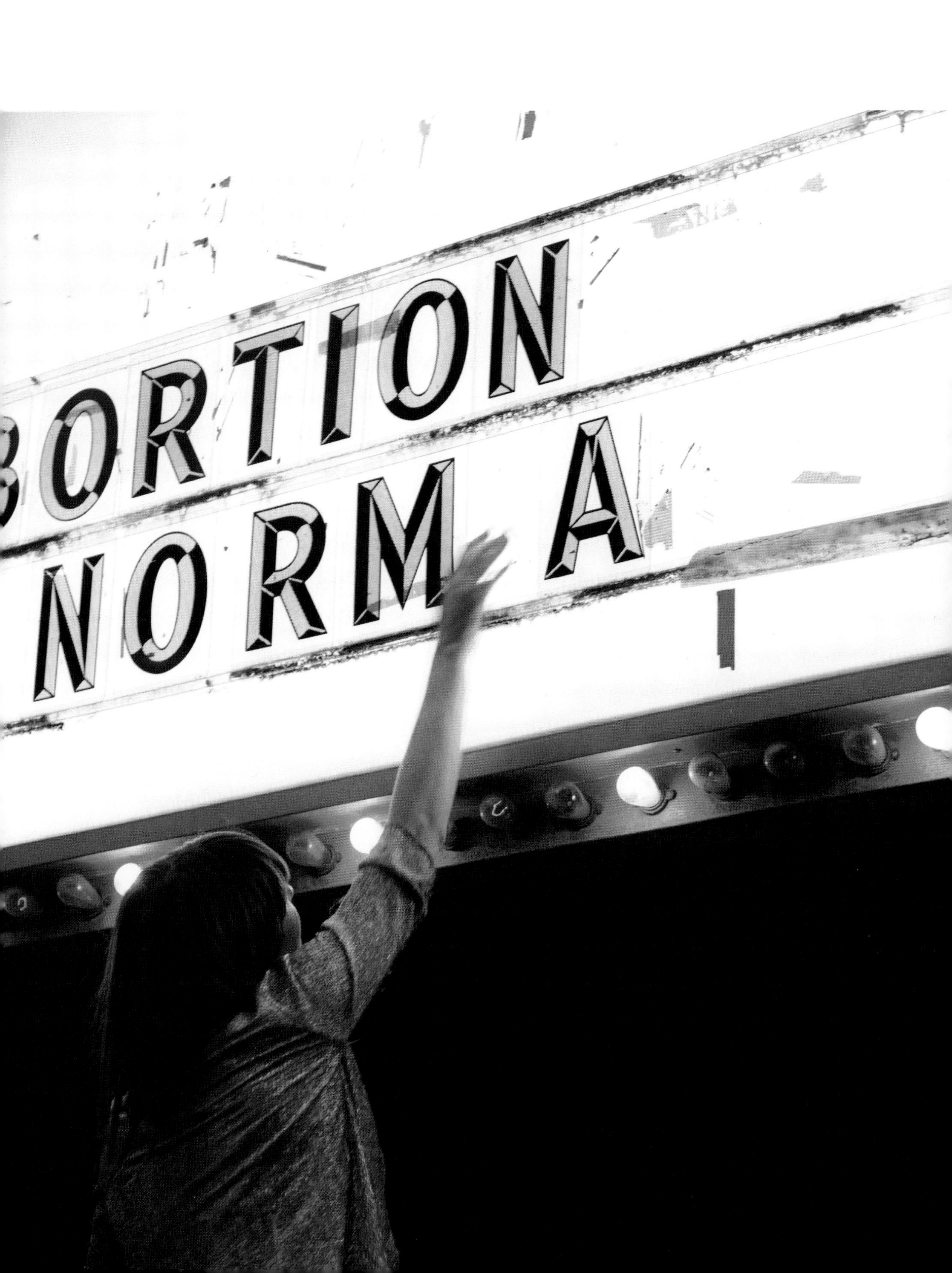
BORTION
NORM A

CHRISSY

In December of 2016 I faced a troubling decision: reclaim my life and salvage what was left or give what little I had to sustaining another. At the time, I'd been coerced into a deeply damaging, physically and mentally abusive relationship with an addict who I was keen on saving. I'd moved to Memphis from a small town in Mississippi one year prior and found myself desperate for friendship, acceptance, and a new shot at life. I was also damaged—I'd been raped twice the previous summer by a man I'd considered a friend. As I struggled to gain approval in a new place, I began to lose myself purposefully. During that time, I met the man who would change my life forever.

I now recognize that he was sexually abusive from the beginning, often shoving his hands down my pants in public and exposing my breasts to his friends. I'd always been a good girl. I wasn't naturally assertive and I'd never been given the tools to fight back. What had happened to me the summer before felt like a loss of dignity, and at that point I had all but given up on loving myself. After he relapsed on heroin, his actions went from aggressively playful to abusive.

At the time, I saw myself as a lost cause. I don't think he saw me as human, often having sex with me while I was asleep and leaving me to deal with the aftermath. I'll never forget finally taking a pregnancy test. I was in complete denial: when you're at the bottom, things can't possibly get worse, right? Fortunately I was with a friend when the results came back. I was in complete disbelief. How could this happen to me? What now?

At that point I was working two jobs and living on my own, barely keeping my head above water. I had been seeking help for my mental health for months, but it wasn't working, and my trauma had led to a drinking problem. I didn't have parents or friends to help me raise a baby. At the time, I didn't feel like I could trust myself to mentally handle childbirth, postpartum health, and raising a child. I couldn't stand the thought of bringing a child into the world and subjecting them to a highly abusive father, like my own had been. The same day I found out I was pregnant, I made an appointment at my local reproductive health center. We went over my options and I decided to have a medication abortion.

As I prepared for my abortion, I knew that I had to find a way out of the relationship. I began brainstorming with a friend, coming up with a number of escape plans. On the day of my abortion, I was alone. I had been through a miscarriage in the past. This time, I was managing my own medically induced miscarriage. Six hours later, it was over, and I finally felt like I could breathe. And in the moments after my abortion, I was reminded of how strong and brave I am. I remembered that I deserve to exist in the world as an autonomous and liberated entity. I knew I'd have another chance to nurture in the future, but that at the time it was imperative that I nurture the woman inside of me that was dying to be free. I left him not long after.

In the two years since my abortion, I've enrolled at the University of Memphis and am now in my senior year studying social sciences. I have become a dedicated advocate for people in need, volunteering with organizations that fight for those who have been abused and sexually assaulted, and helping people understand that survival is possible. I am a patient advocate with CHOICES Reproductive Health Services in Memphis, I'm an abortion doula, and I've visited the state capitol to advocate for reproductive rights.

The ability to make choices for ourselves is critical.

If I hadn't been able to make an autonomous decision about my body and well-being, I would be dead. And as it turns out, choosing not to be a mother has allowed me to heal myself and nurture others in a way I never thought possible. ■

DANIELLE CAMPOAMOR

When I look at my son, I think about abortion.

His crooked smile reminds me of the receptionist at the Bellingham, Washington, Planned Parenthood, sandwiched between Ellis and York Streets. The way he reaches his small, pudgy hands toward mine as we approach a crosswalk reminds me of the nurse's hand I held during my seven-minute surgical abortion; her gentle, subtle squeezes letting me know that I wasn't alone, it was almost over, and I was doing great. The way he says, "I love you, Momma," reminds me of the profound love I had for myself when I was 23 and decided that I mattered more than an unplanned pregnancy, more than a zygote, and more than my country's patriarchal expectations.

WITHOUT ABORTION, MY SON WOULD NOT EXIST.

My son's room, filled with books, stuffed animals, and action figures, reminds me of my overwhelming privilege as a white-passing Puerto Rican woman living in a liberal state. I didn't have to endure a mandatory waiting period, forced counseling, or a required ultrasound in order to take my future back. I didn't have to travel long distances or find money to pay for an overnight hotel stay or research transportation options in order to walk into a clinic that provides safe, legal, affordable abortions. I didn't have to hide my decision from my mother or my partner, and I assumed I didn't have to hide it from my friends.

My son's first hospital visit, when he was almost one year old, after I had carelessly turned my back for a second, forced me to recall the moment I came dangerously close to killing myself to prove I deserved the life I chose. My back alley was the cultural stigma of abortion. My coat hanger was the judgment, the shame, and the near-constant verbal attacks from distant anti-choice family members, friends, and internet strangers. I was a murderer. I was going to hell. I was worthless. I didn't deserve to live. I should die. All spewed in my direction via callous social-media posts and long-winded emails and factually inaccurate memes shared continuously, endlessly, and without remorse.

My son's fanatic love of cars reminds me of the night I got in my own after drinking at a local bar. My son's make-believe pileups with Lego cars and monster trucks reminds me of the moment I turned down a dirt road, driving 30 miles per hour over the speed limit, and flipped my car three times before landing on the roof, my head hitting the windshield and knocking me unconscious as my seatbelt strap cut into my chest.

The lazy way my son wakes up every morning reminds me of the moment I woke up hanging upside down in my totaled vehicle. The moment I realized I deserved a future devoid of shame and judgment and prescribed guilt. The moment I couldn't continue self-destructing to appease people who despise the freedom, sexuality, and bodily autonomy of women. The moment I decided to no longer apologize for loving myself more than an unplanned pregnancy, a zygote, and anyone else's expectations.

My son's annual trips to his kind, caring, and understanding pediatrician cannot help but revive the undeniable fact that the shame and stigma of abortion care almost killed me before I got the chance to be his mother.

My son's all-consuming, innate need for me reminds me of how dangerously close I came to never having him at all.

My son's temper tantrums and potty-training accidents and late-night wakeup calls and defiant tendencies and boundary-testing declarations remind me of how all-consuming, overwhelming, beautiful, difficult, fulfilling, terrifying, and incredible motherhood truly is. And if we are to continue to hold up motherhood as a beautiful life choice, then we, as a nation, cannot position parenthood as a punishment.

My son is not my condemnation for being a sexual being. My son is not the manifestation of "making the best of a worst-case scenario." My son is not a consequence legislated by rich, white, Christian men. My son is a choice—my choice—made when I was ready, willing, and able to be his mother and as a direct result of easy, affordable access to abortion care.

When I look at my son, I think about abortion. Because without abortion, my son would not exist. ■

NEVER HIDE
Abortion

EMILY

I found out I was pregnant in the summer of 2013, a few weeks before my 21st birthday. I was about to enter my senior year of college, and I was hopelessly in love.

I had been dating my boyfriend for about a year and a half, and our relationship was volatile and unhealthy by pretty much all standards. Even so, I would have followed him to the end of the earth. I remember sitting outside his dorm room in the dead of Upstate New York winter, waiting for him to be done berating me and let me back in so I could sleep on the floor of his closet. Yeah, it was degrading as fuck. I could have gone back to my own dorm room, but I never did. I just loved this man so damn much, I was scared that if I walked away—even just to the warmth of my bed for the night—I'd lose him forever. He made sure I knew that, at any point, one wrong move on my part and he'd be gone. That's how he got away with doing pretty much anything he pleased. Manipulation, fear, and pain coursed through our relationship.

I PROBABLY COULD HAVE HAD AN OKAY LIFE IF I HAD CHOSEN TO CONTINUE MY PREGNANCY. BUT I DIDN'T WANT TO.

Despite all this, I saw myself with him forever. I told myself we would make it work. He would learn to be kinder. I would learn to be more accepting. He was really sweet sometimes, I told myself. He made me *feel*, I told myself. I wanted to graduate together, go out in the world together, and eventually have a family together. And I almost had that.

Looking back, I realize that getting pregnant could have sealed our fate, binding me forever to this man who wasn't good for me, a man with whom I was weak—a shell of the woman I am today. But when I did get pregnant, I knew that I couldn't commit. Ultimately, this unplanned pregnancy was one of the most pivotal and empowering moments in my life.

I wanted an abortion as soon as I saw the two lines on the pregnancy test. Despite my pipe dreams about living happily ever after together, reality hit when I learned I was pregnant. I couldn't have a child with this man! Suddenly, having an abortion was the obvious choice. Essentially powerless in my relationship, I was powerless no more.

Having an abortion reminded me that I was the one in control of my life—that despite the powerlessness I had felt for the last year and a half, I *did* have power; I *could* determine the direction of my life. I stood a little taller and walked with more conviction. I was doing something for myself! I was making a decision that was *good for me*.

With just a little more confidence, I broke up with my boyfriend soon after the abortion. I moved on, rediscovered my self-worth, and met someone who has shown me a truer meaning of love. I'm marrying him this fall, and we want to have a baby as soon as possible.

The truth is, no matter if I had chosen abortion, adoption, or parenting, my life probably would have turned out okay. But that's not the point. We women are so damn resilient that sometimes it backfires; our ability to make do in nearly any situation is often at the expense of our own wants and needs. Yeah, I probably could have made do and had an okay life if I had chosen to continue my pregnancy. But I didn't want to. ■

JOYELLE NICOLE JOHNSON

I got pregnant the classy way: on the floor of a handicap bathroom on an Amtrak train. And if you're having sex on the floor of a handicap bathroom on an Amtrak train... then maybe you aren't ready to be a mother. (I'm not judging anyone but me and my college boyfriend—if you like to get it on in bathrooms, on floors, or on trains, more power to you!) As soon as we were finished, I had a strange feeling. Something was different. I instantly knew that I was pregnant, and my suspicions were confirmed a few weeks later.

At the time, I was a junior in college and had been seeing my boyfriend for a year. That was going great. My family, on the other hand, was a hot mess. Folks were dying and getting sick in what seemed like droves. As a matter of fact, the "pregnancy express" had been headed to a funeral for one of my closest cousins who had died suddenly, the day before his 19th birthday. The autopsy was inconclusive. And, to add more fuel to the fuckery fire, 9/11 had happened the month before, the day before my birthday, and I'm from a town in New Jersey right across the Hudson River. Needless to say, that whole year sucked a huge D for me. My boyfriend and I hadn't used a condom, and I blame my recklessness on a traumatic state of mind: I had zero fucks to give about anything. The sky was falling, and I was Chicken Little.

I'M A BETTER PERSON FOR REMOVING THAT MICROSCOPIC CLUMP OF CELLS BEFORE IT BECAME A HUMAN LIFE.

When I found out I was pregnant, I became significantly more overwhelmed. I was attending Boston College, a Jesuit institution that didn't give access to birth control on campus but did allow Cardinal Law—a priest infamous for his role in suppressing allegations of sexual assault within the church—to give commencement speeches. I love my alma mater but... man. Also, I had to tell my mother. My boyfriend was too scared to tell his, but my mother was a labor and delivery nurse who'd met my "father" (I put that in quotes because he wasn't much of a father to me) at UMDNJ hospital in Newark, New Jersey. He was an OB-GYN (yes, my deadbeat dad was a successful doctor) whose specialty was—wait for it—abortions. So I knew when it came time to tell her she wouldn't be mad. Especially considering she's the most peaceful person I've ever met in my life, like if Mother Teresa had been born in the projects of Brooklyn.

Still, I was teary-eyed when I made the phone call. "Mommy, I'm pregnant." Her response, "Well... what do you want to do?" Choice. It was as simple as that. She had my back.

She offered a few options, like me having the baby in the summer and finishing school while she raised her grandchild for the first year. Her level of altruism is unparalleled. But I knew I couldn't do that to my mother, my child, or myself. The guilt alone would've crushed me. So I chose to have an abortion. Guilt-free.

A little background on my parents: not one but both of them have indicated to me that I was an accident. My "father" once callously blurted, "I told your mother to have an abortion. What do you want from me?" And my mother once fleetingly mentioned that she was on her way to abort me but decided not to go through with it on a whim. While altruistic, she's not always the most tactful. So here I am.

Mommy had an old family friend do the procedure, and fortunately he put me to sleep. Translation: I had a fancy rich-lady abortion. I was alone that day, though. My mom happened to be out of town, and my man didn't come because, like I said, he was scared to tell his mommy. In his defense, she had the temperament of a Disney villain, so I kind of understood, but deal with it—you're not even the one on the table! Conveniently, men don't actually have to deal with abortion at all, which is why they shouldn't have a damn thing to say about what I do with my body.

My cousin dropped me off. When I was about to go under, I was sobbing uncontrollably, and the doctor stopped and asked, "Do you want to do this?" "Yes," I answered, in between heaves. And then I woke up, alone, to zero regrets. I'm a better person for removing that microscopic clump of cells before it became a human life.

I sometimes think about how the child would be 14 now. That thought doesn't make me sad, though. I definitely want to have a baby or two—when the time is right. And I'm happy to live in a country where I had that choice. ■

JOY

It is hard for me to write about my abortions because I want to defend my decisions... but I am also so very angry that these decisions, above all others, seem to require defense.

I can tell you that I was too young to be a parent when I got pregnant for the first time during my freshman year of college. I can tell you that I had severe postpartum depression after the birth of my first child, and had very real reasons to think that giving birth to any additional children would do serious damage to my mental health, as well as damage to my marriage and to my ability to parent the child I already had. I can tell you about the failures of multiple birth control methods.

Or I can tell you that I simply didn't want to give birth to any children except the one that I had.

My first abortion, at age 18, was surgical, and it was more physically difficult and invasive than all the subsequent terminations, which were done by pill. But the first one was also—by definition—my only abortion, and there was comfort in believing that it would always be my only. One mistake can happen to anyone. Plus, I was 18.

Sixteen or so years later, I finally had my second accident. That decision was harder. I found out I was pregnant when hCG hormones were detected in a blood test taken to diagnose something entirely unrelated to reproduction, on a Monday in June, on my husband's first day at a new job. The next day, a beloved family member was diagnosed with lung cancer. The day after that, Wednesday, our computer crashed, taking the first three months of my daughter's baby photos with it. On Thursday I was told I was being let go from my job as an attorney.

Did I mention the postpartum depression, the unresolved health issues that had me getting blood tests in the first place, and that fact that my husband and I were, in fact, using condoms correctly and consistently? It was not a good week. And yet, it was a difficult decision. I didn't want to be a woman who has multiple abortions. One is a mistake; two is a pattern. Plus, I was 34, happily married, living in a three-bedroom apartment, and doing pretty well financially—even when taking the layoff into account. If we wanted to, we could have made it work. But I didn't want to.

MY ONLY FLEETING REGRET WAS THAT I WAS BRIEFLY MADE TO FEEL LIKE I SHOULD REGRET CHOOSING THE COURSE OF MY OWN LIFE.

In the end, it was that simple. And my following three unwanted pregnancies were hardly decisions at all. We had already decided that we were a family of three, and we planned to stay that way.

I am incredibly grateful to my husband, who said he didn't give a shit what anyone thought (even hypothetically) and that we should—I should—do what made us happy. I am grateful to my best friend, also 34 and married, but who very much wanted a second child of her own, who got the "I'm pregnant" phone call and still responded, "I… is that a good thing, or not so much?" And I am grateful to Planned Parenthood, who only wanted to know if I was making the decision while of sound mind and without unwanted pressure.

The thing that pisses me off most about people who would judge me for my abortions is the utter lack of respect it displays for the child and family I actually have. If I had continued with my pregnancy back in college, I would not have my daughter, this daughter. Even if I'd had more hypothetical children in that alternate universe, it is mathematically certain that her life would not have come into being. And keeping any of the unplanned—and unwanted—pregnancies that followed her birth would have changed me as a parent, and therefore changed her life as well.

Why is that hypothetical child more valuable than the one that exists at this very real moment? I am a woman who has had multiple abortions.

It turns out, that changes me not at all. People who read this may judge me, but the ones who meet me in real life would never see it coming. I'm not irresponsible, a child-hater, or any of the things they say about those who are pro-choice and those who have abortions. I'm still happily married, still blissfully a mom. My only fleeting regret was that I was briefly made to feel like I should regret choosing the course of my own life.

Fuck that noise, am I right? ■

a balloon rises and pops

somewhere deep inside my chest

where I am still a child, the virgin

but also

a crone, traversing thick blue woods

there is three of me

the other, the maiden, cries out in protest

they raise their voices in a chorus

shrill

sweet

and cacophonous in their disagreement

"ladies, ladies"

I joke

"there is enough to go around,"

this cake is not fit for your tender maws just yet

I will bury it in the front yard

where the rain will soak it through and an invisible thing will grow

outside of me

–LILA BONOW (2018)

CASSANDRA PANEK

I was 23, fresh out of college and working part-time at a craft store. My partner and I had been friends for years before our relationship became something more, which felt promising but uncertain. We lived in the same house with about 15 roommates, and most of our free time and resources were focused on drinking and exploring our vices.

I'd been off hormonal birth control since graduating and losing access to student health services. I was relying on condoms as a sole means of protection, which made me nervous—I'm a person who likes redundancy and multiple layers of security. I was looking into an IUD, trying to figure out how I could afford it, and I made an appointment at Planned Parenthood to discuss my options. But my prescreening pregnancy test informed me that I was a few weeks too late.

My partner and I had already discussed our feelings about reproduction, which made the situation more straightforward. We each leaned toward not wanting children at all—certainly not now, when our lives were nothing more than working and drinking. Even if we wanted to (which we were pretty certain we didn't), we'd only been together for four months and there was no guarantee we'd still be involved in another nine. We weren't suited to be parents; we were barely functioning as adults. When I learned I was pregnant, we revisited our previous conversation and decided that we still felt the same. I scheduled the procedure.

At this time, Pennsylvania had a waiting period and other criteria to have an abortion. As if the situation isn't stressful enough, you're up against a time limit and other arbitrary restrictions that hinder your ability to get the care you need in a timely fashion. I'd faced the possibility of unwanted pregnancy since I started having sex at 17. Abortion wasn't a decision I made quickly or lightly; it was something I thought about every month, in the anxious day or two before I got my period. An extra 24 or 48 hours wasn't going to influence my decision, but it could influence my treatment options.

AN EXTRA 48 HOURS WASN'T GOING TO INFLUENCE MY DECISION, BUT IT COULD INFLUENCE MY TREATMENT OPTIONS.

I'm grateful that I had the means and mobility to get to a clinic in New Jersey instead, which didn't have the waiting period. They scheduled my appointment quickly and with no grief; we discussed my options without any judgment or stigma. They treated abortion like any other outpatient procedure, and me like any other patient making an informed choice for my personal health. I had my abortion with minimal stress, and as soon as my menstrual cycle returned to normal, I was able to get my IUD—thanks again to my local Planned Parenthood.

It's been 10 years. I turned 34 last week, and I'm grateful for the life I'm living, made possible by a single, safe, legal medical procedure. I'm grateful for a supportive, communicative partner, who helped me scrape together the money necessary for an abortion in a hurry—10 years ago, that $400 was one of our rent payments for an entire month. If finding that money was hard, how impossible would it have been for us to support an additional human?

My same partner and I are still together. We've been married for four years and have a very nice dog, which was the final step in our decision to never have children. I have health insurance now, and at my next gyno checkup I'll be deciding whether to get a fresh IUD, or if I'm finally a candidate for something permanent. ■

CLAUDIA & JO ANNE

Claudia: First, let's talk about your abortion, Mom. How did you find out? What'd they even do back then?

Jo Anne: Well, the interesting thing is that I had two abortions.

Claudia: Oh my God! I only knew about the one!

Jo Anne: Well there you go! I had one before *Roe v. Wade*, and then one after. And I was just thinking about this before I got here... between my mother, me, you, and your daughter Isabelle, we are four generations of women who have been in therapy and we've really analyzed a lot of abortions in there. Actually, I remember my mother telling me that she was "an abortion that didn't take." She was the fourth child of six.

Claudia: Grandma told me this story when she was like 80 years old! They'd tried to do some kind of at-home abortion, and I'm not sure what happened, but as my grandmother put it, "Ho, ho, ho, boy was everyone surprised when I showed up!"

Jo Anne: That was in 1915. And she almost died. Her father took care of her afterward while her mother was recovering. And the way they both told it, it really was an important event in my grandfather's life—feeling like he cared for this baby daughter of his, after her abortion didn't take.

Back to my story. Starting with the first one, the illegal one. It was 1950, and I was a single mom with a four-year-old daughter. I'd met this man in acting school, and I up and left my first husband, Claudia's father, because I just wanted to live my life. I really believed that.

I blame this first pregnancy on bad doctoring, which I got from the doctor who delivered Claudia. And he was a very famous doctor! He not only delivered Claudia, but also delivered Barbra Streisand's children.

Claudia: What??

Jo Anne: Yep. Anyway, I went to see him with some kind of infection. He was South African and very handsome, and very, very flirtatious—actually, he hit on me! But he told me, "You can't get pregnant because you've got this infection, so don't worry about it." I was seeing Mark at the time—he's now Claudia's stepfather—and because of what the doctor said, we didn't think we needed to use contraceptives. And then I didn't get my period. I just panicked. This was 1950. There were no solutions if you didn't have money, and even if you had money, you would go to Puerto Rico and go into a back door. And I had no solutions.

Claudia: And also, everyone was already mad at you, because you'd left your husband to be with someone else, and you were an unmarried single mother. I know your mother was mad at you.

Jo Anne: Everybody was mad at me. I left the rich, garment-center dressmaker's son, just to do what I wanted to do. As I mentioned earlier, in our family, everybody went to therapy. If you had a problem in our household, the solution was to go to a mental institution. At this time, I hadn't slept for three days, I had no money, I was pregnant, and everybody was mad at me. So I checked into a loony bin for 10 days. It was over Christmas, and there were a lot of interesting alcoholics who you could go into the bathroom and smoke with. It was all right. And thank God the man I had fallen in love with, the love of my life, he was a standup guy. He came and visited me in the loony bin, and he said, "I've got a solution." When I got home, he'd arranged for an abortion. He had a friend, a waiter at a comedy club in Sheepshead Bay. There was a lovely woman there named Rita who worked part-time as a nurse and part-time as a short-order cook, and she was a midget. And Rita agreed to do the abortion.

Claudia: I think the term now is "little person."

Jo Anne: Got it, little person. Well, Rita was a great little person. She performed my abortion in the apartment that we were living in, and two of my friends were there. I didn't suffer physically at the time. But I didn't pass the whole pregnancy, and then there was an infection. I had to go back to that bad doctor, and he did a D&C. I was lucky. He was ultimately not so lucky. He ended up dying in that big Korean Airlines crash. Anyway, that was the first abortion.

Claudia: And when did you have the second one?

Jo Anne: This one happened when you were 11 or 12. I think that there must have been a hole in my diaphragm. But the abortion was so simple! There was a Planned Parenthood clinic four or five blocks away from where we lived. Mark and I went over, and they did one of those vacuum cleaner events and it was... fine. We didn't feel we had the finances, we weren't ready to have a child, and we just made the choice. There was no need to make it a drama. It was just a decision made by two adults.

All right, Claudia, your turn. Do you have an abortion story to tell me?

Claudia: I do! I was 23 or 24. I had been sober for just a little while. I was with my daughter's father, and we hadn't been together that long. It wasn't an ideal time. I was financially struggling, but the main thing was that I was in what could be called the panic-disorder period of my life. As you know, my daughter's father was... well, whatever. We don't need to go into that. When I got pregnant, it was a little bit of a decision because he already had a daughter, who I loved. He felt pretty confident about his parenting skills, and he was 15 years older than me. But I was in a difficult period. I remember talking to you and Mark about it. And you basically said, "Well, it sounds like this is not the right time for you to have a child." And I agreed, and that was that.

And the abortion itself couldn't have been simpler. It was covered by my insurance, which I still had from the Screen Actors Guild. My doctor was the best. They gave me a Valium drip, and then the vacuum cleaner situation.

It wasn't an easy decision. And I think it probably has more emotion around it now that I've had a child. But now I just sort of think, "Well, we weren't ready for Isabella."

Jo Anne: I mean, the whole point of all this is choice. Mark and I thought about having children again, once you were a teenager, and we had done well after he'd worked his ass off, and he wanted to have a child. And I said no. I just wanted to be free to develop my career, my artistic side. And Mark thought about it and he said, "I respect that choice."

Claudia: It's a lot to ask a person to house another person inside their body, you know? I always knew I wanted exactly one.

Jo Anne: Me too! Isn't that interesting about the two of us? I wanted one and I wanted it to be a girl.

Claudia: I felt the same way. I think I just wanted to do everything you did. But you know, I didn't love being pregnant. I actually hated it. I was very physically uncomfortable. Then you have a baby, which is no walk in the park. Motherhood is great, but you should only do it if you want to. I'm always telling my friends: if you don't want to do this, you'll be fine. You can have a great life, there are lots of babies around you, and not everybody has to have a child! Don't feel guilty. You know yourself and what you can handle.

Jo Anne: I agree. Whatever you decide is okay. But the key is being able to make a choice, and we have to protect that. ■

Jo Anne Astrow has been in show business most of her life: acting, producing, and performing comedy and improv. Her daughter Claudia Lonow Rapaport has written, acted, directed, performed stand-up, and raised a daughter of her own. This conversation took place (on stage, of course) at the Improv in Hollywood, which is co-owned by Claudia's husband Mark.

SHELLY BELL

LOVE in 40 Nontraditional, Unpredictable Steps

1. It's June 29, 2013. I host the "I Am Slam" in the Adams Morgan neighborhood in Washington, D.C. as a part of the Songwriters and Poets Series.

2. We go out for drinks.

3. After getting the fun type of drunk, my entourage and I find our final dance destination.

4. I see Paul on the dance floor. My version of this story includes fans blowing my hair, a spotlight, and catching eyes with the geekiest guy on the floor. In reality, he was a dark-chocolate muscle-bound dream come true.

5. We dance all night. He is the only person I dance with.

6. We exchange numbers. He kisses me. That's weird. We're black! We don't get drunk and kiss strangers in the club! Oh well, we're drunk!

7. I drunk call him later. He says, "Can I come over?" In a dramatic, whiny voice I say, "I don't know, I don't usually do this. (I don't!) If you come over are you going to try to have sex with me?" He says, "We'll just let whatever happens happen." Typical guy thing to say.

8. He comes over. Of course we have sex.

9. We wake up. I look over and he is still in my bed. I'm thinking, "Dude! Aren't these called one-night stands because you should be standing and walking away by now?"

10. I give him the fake wake-up stretch/loud yawn. He rolls over like we're chilling!

11. According to his story, I gave him like two different reasons he had to leave. I just remember that I wanted him to get out.

12. We agree to keep in touch. He finally rolls out.

13. Life goes on. I don't call him, he doesn't call me.

ONE MONTH LATER

14. My mood swings are particularly strong, pizza makes me sick, and my breasts grow huge and tender.

15. There's a stomach virus going around, so I assume my nausea to be the virus claiming me as the next victim.

16. But I'm not sure. So I go to the dollar store, purchase a pregnancy test, take it, and yeah... it's positive.

17. I'm totally shocked and feeling crazy! I haven't talked to this dude since the night we hooked up, and I also haven't had sex with anyone else. I'm filled with anxiety. How am I supposed to call this random guy named Paul and tell him I'm pregnant?

18. I text him first like, "Heeyy, remember me? That girl from the club?" He replies excitedly, "HEY! I'm glad to hear from you. My roommate just asked about you. I lost your number. Call me."

19. I call. "Hey! So, I need to talk to you. Umm, I've been feeling sick lately. I went to the dollar store, purchased a test, and it's positive. I'm going to Walmart now to purchase another test and will let you know what happens."

20. He is surprisingly super cool about it! "Okay, call me back after you come back from Walmart."

21. I am freaking out the entire time! I feel extremely guilty about getting pregnant by some random guy in a club.

22. Of course the Walmart test is positive.

23. I text him the news. He says, "Okay, let's just talk about it." I am now beginning to think he is a little weird. I had expected a huge dramatic "it ain't mine" fiasco upon contacting him. That didn't happen.

24. I get an ultrasound. They tell me the date of conception is June 30. I'm totally pregnant and it's totally Paul's!

25. I ask him why he's being so cool about it. He says that he's seen friends and family members freak in a situation like this and then find out the child *was* theirs, creating a messed-up situation for everybody involved.

26. At some point in the "what are we going to do about this?" conversation, we agree to move forward with an abortion on the grounds that we will continue to see each other. If we like each other, we'll plan to have another child. Sounded like a deal to me! I didn't want my baby's story to be, "Oh yeah, I was being a whore, and you're the beauty that came from that!" SMH.

27. The night before the abortion, we go to dinner. We just hang out, laugh, and talk.

28. On the day of the abortion, he comes with me to the clinic. They call my name. I go to empty my bladder. While in the bathroom, I text him asking, "Are you sure you want to do this?" He responds, "No."

29. I reply, "What?! Why didn't you tell me? I'm not sure I want to do it either."

30. I beg the nurse for five minutes to go back into the lobby. She lets me go.

31. Paul is sitting in a waiting room chair near the door. I look him in the eye and ask, "Are you sure?" He says, "No, but this is what we agreed to do. I just don't want you to resent me after this. I still want to see you."

32. I assure him that I won't resent him. We remind ourselves that this is what we agreed to do. I turn to walk away. He grabs my arm, pulls me close, and kisses me.

33. The abortion happens.

34. The next week I go to Miami for a friend's birthday. The week I come back, *he* goes to Miami to celebrate *his* birthday. We barely keep in touch.

35. Randomly, the night of a Cowboys v. Redskins game, I get a text from Paul saying, "Clear your schedule Saturday. I want to see you."

36. Who does he think he is, texting me and demanding my time like that? No, I didn't say that. I was like, "Okay!" (LOL.)

37. The next Saturday, we go to Red Lobster. We talk openly about the abortion and how it made us feel. We laugh, we talk, we have special moments in conversation about the decision we made. We both feel a certain level of guilt. We both feel like if we'd only known that the person we had a one-night stand with was this great a person, we would have been proud to keep the baby.

38. After that, we fall in love in a way neither of us could ever have imagined happening. We've been seeing each other ever since.

39. In November 2013, we start trying to have a baby.

40. The second time is the charm. This is my nontraditional fairytale love story. Our relationship feels something close to perfect: there are rollercoaster rides, laughs, hugs, tears, and passion. The kids love him, and he loves the kids. We disagree like all couples do. We are dedicated to learning each other like all couples should be. Ultimately, Paul was the missing piece of my family puzzle. ■

ABORTION
IS NORMAL

SHAWNA MURPHY

I've been pro-choice for as long as I can remember. I was always the one who had to take on the young Republicans in debate club, with their "pro-life" bullshit. But I never got pregnant. I was on the pill before I even started having sex. When I was young, some of my friends had abortions; it just wasn't something that happened to me.

I was a nanny for years and relied on Planned Parenthood for birth control and lady biz because I never had insurance. When I became a childcare director and was finally able to afford insurance, I was really proud. I felt like a grown up, like I'd finally arrived. I chose a primary health care provider and started actually going to the doctor for things unrelated to my vagina.

Then, at 29 years old, I met the man who would later become my husband, and he was really good at getting me pregnant. The first time, the condom broke. I was worried I might get pregnant so I called my new, fancy primary care provider for help. She declined to see me, so I was stuck, calling around to local pharmacies looking for morning-after contraceptives in the days before cell phones. My car happened to be in the shop, so I took two buses to get to a pharmacy that would sell me the morning-after pill without a doctor's note.

I spent the next 24 hours sicker than sick, doing whatever it was to my uterus that those pills do. I didn't tell anyone other than my man. Even though I didn't feel like I was doing something wrong, I was so attached to how others might view my choices that I kept the physical pain I was experiencing to myself.

A few years later, we got pregnant for real. We were married and I had always wanted to be a mother, but the timing was just . . . well, wrong. I had been depressed; I felt like I was drinking too much—we couldn't afford a baby, let alone childcare. I called that "primary care provider" again. This time she flat-out refused to see me. I called my old standby, Planned Parenthood. They got me in and gave me medication to terminate my pregnancy. They were kind, friendly, competent, and maybe even a tad over-supportive since I wasn't feeling in the least bit emotional about my choice to terminate.

I took a long weekend from work. My husband rented me a stack of trashy DVDs (*The Osbornes*, I think), and I took two pills: something to make me miscarry and something for the pain. It was the worst. I remember throwing up and being on the toilet as the pregnancy was wrenched out of me. Physically, it *really* hurt. But I never regretted it or second-guessed my choice. I also really didn't tell anyone. My husband knew, and maybe one coworker and a few very close friends. Otherwise, I was very guarded about my abortion. I think back now and wonder why. Maybe it was because I have always been such a mother. Maybe I worried it wouldn't make sense to people, because everyone knew I wanted to have children and I didn't want to explain why the timing just wasn't right.

Shortly thereafter, I got pregnant again, and she was the *one*. My husband and I were elated. I had my first baby in 2004. After her, we knew we wanted to have one more. I got pregnant again and miscarried, then got pregnant again and miscarried again. It was traumatic to say the least. I woke up in the middle of the night holding my three-year-old, soaking in blood. I drove with my husband in a borrowed Jeep, as my body tried to expel a tiny fetus in a tiny sac. I ended up in the ER getting filled with fluids. I owed nearly $3,000 in medical bills, and I had no baby to show for it.

We finally had our second baby. She is glorious and worth all the work. We came to believe that our five pregnancies—two live births, two miscarriages, and one choice to terminate—all these things led to us having the babies we were meant to have. And still, we only talked about it late at night, in hushed tones, with each other.

When Planned Parenthood and abortion in general came under attack in 2015, I realized I couldn't be silent any longer. I could no longer be private. I remember making a Facebook post about my abortion and getting a lot of support. I knew that I had to be a part of normalizing women's experiences of sex, birth, miscarriage, and abortion. I started trying to talk about my own experiences with my women friends and was surprised how many others had had abortions too. And yet we remained silent and private.

For my 47th birthday, I asked my family to attend Shout Your Abortion's Stomp the Patriarchy Ball at Seattle's Washington Hall. I knew they normally would've never acquiesced—it was the Friday of the first week of school and we were all completely fried. But it was my birthday, and they love me, so they got it together, put on their best outfits, and we went.

Attending the event with my family meant I had to explain abortion to my 12-year-old. She was not having it. Despite my best efforts, she thought it sounded horrific. Hoping to finally make a breakthrough, I told her that I'd had an abortion. This was earth-shattering to her. But we attended the event, and my oldest had the time of her life. On her own, she managed to meet Congresswoman Jayapal and had a great discussion about how she didn't feel like abortion was a choice she would like to make, but that she wanted it to be safe and available for all women. My lesbian 12-year-old! On one of her many trips to the bathroom she also met Lelah Maupin from Tacocat, who performed that night. By the end of the evening she had come to the realization that I had made the right choice for me and that she was proud of me for being honest and comfortable with my decisions about my body.

For me, this is huge. My lesbian 12-year-old, who can't picture herself getting pregnant accidentally because she knows she will probably have to go pretty far out of her way to get knocked up! She understands my body, my choice. For me, that means that she will also grow up believing that she can make her own choices for her body, and that other women are entitled to those choices too. I want her to grow up knowing that having sex, getting pregnant, miscarrying, and terminating pregnancies are all normal parts of women's experiences. And I hope that both of my daughters can grow up knowing they can choose to be silent or private or loud. I hope they don't always have to be loud, but I will be. For them. ■

Shout Your
ABORTION!
THIS IS NOT A DEBATE.

EMILY ELIZABETH

Thinking about my abortions calls up a complex suite of emotions: relief, nostalgia, gratitude, anger, pride. I'm writing this in my cozy living room, sipping wine after a couple of outstanding days, listening to my cat purring next to me on the couch. Recalling each emotion and examining them is work; there's no way around that. But underneath that examination, I feel a calm, solid sense of peace and strength.

The year 2015 was my year of abortions. I'd been in an abusive marriage for four years, and he finally managed to get me pregnant a few months before we planned to move from Houston to San Francisco. Texas is not kind to women seeking abortions, or to uterus owners at large, for that matter. I was the sole breadwinner in my unhealthy little family, and affording a procedure in Houston seemed impossible, so I sped up the move to California, where Planned Parenthood offered the service for free based on my negligible income. I was on the West Coast for one day before my appointment.

BECAUSE I WAS ABLE TO CONTROL MY BODY, MY LIFE HAS CHANGED FOR THE BETTER.

My then-husband and I took a Lyft to the clinic where I'd chosen to have the medication abortion, but after the appointment, he made me walk over three miles. The antibiotic the clinic had given me upset my stomach, and I fought the urge to vomit every step I took through the city. I now understand that I was being punished for standing up for myself because he didn't want me to have the abortion. The night before, he'd tried to talk me out of it. I'll never forget the way he badgered me. We were in some woods, and he was telling me how "glorious our son will be." The way he ignored the daughter he already had stuck in my head. I didn't let him change my mind.

The next day, I took the misoprostol. I wasn't really prepared for the pain. For several hours, I bled and cramped, but when it was over, it was over. The fear and uncertainty I'd been feeling were gone. I had taken control of my future for the first time in years, and it felt powerful.

I left my husband later that year, but not before he tried again to sink his hooks into me using another unwanted pregnancy. Despite his wheedling and name-calling, I scheduled another abortion with Planned Parenthood. This time, I chose the surgical procedure, and I went in alone. The staff was compassionate and didn't even let on how ridiculous my outfit was. (Pro-tip: don't wear cute tights and shorts to your abortion, you will regret it, no matter how adorable you look.) Within a couple of hours, I was finished. The discomfort was minimal. And once again, I didn't feel like the murderer my ex-husband tried to tell me I was. I felt confident and strong. I felt like my own person, in charge of who and what I was. And I never regretted my decisions for an instant.

I was lucky. I had the support of most of the people who mattered to me—with the exception of my ex-husband and a former friend who'd told me that God wouldn't love me anymore. My chosen family understood and held me when I needed it most. The person who was my rock during that difficult time is still my rock today, and our love for each other is deeper and more brilliant than ever. But I was so lucky.

People get abortions for all sorts of reasons, but one thing unites us: a desire to regulate our own bodies, to shape our own futures. My abortions were difficult because of the circumstances surrounding them. But my abortions made me strong. They were catalysts to my realizing that I had agency, that I could choose my path, that I was the one who knew myself and what I wanted best. They taught me that I am a force, and they made me feel free.

Because I was able to control my body, my life has changed for the better. I currently volunteer with a local nonprofit that helps people seeking abortions in Texas get to their appointments. People sometimes come from hours away, needing rides, financial support, and someplace safe to stay overnight in order to comply with the waiting period in Texas.

It's not that I want everyone to have an abortion; I want everyone to be able to make that decision for themselves. I feel an affinity for others who have faced the absurd stigma associated with choosing one's own health and life over an unwanted pregnancy, and those who chose to respect themselves despite being told they don't deserve respect. And I am so sad and angry for the people who don't have that opportunity.

No one knows what is right for your body and your future except you. ■

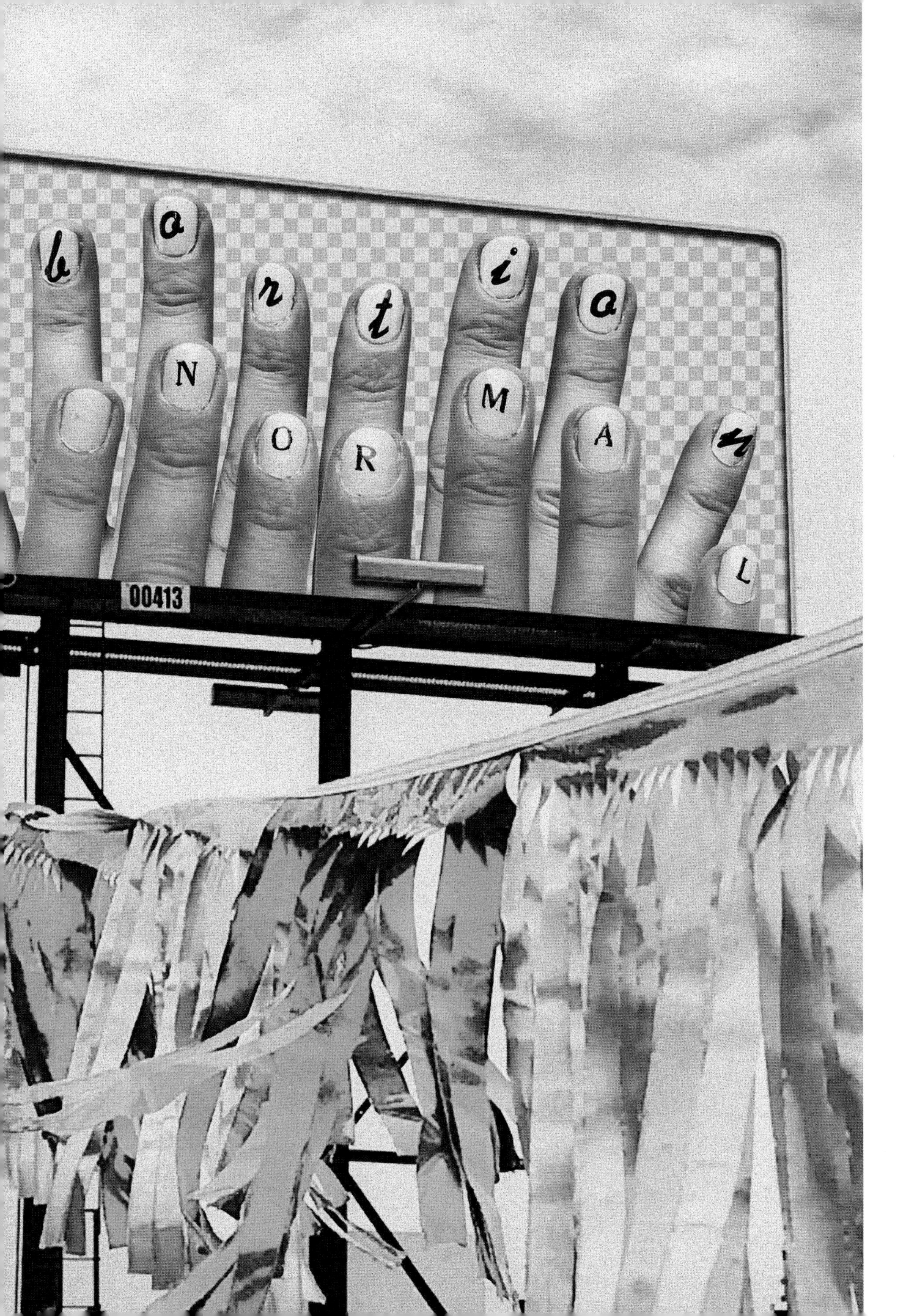
NORMAL
00413

AJA DAILEY

When I was 17 years old, I decided to get an IUD. Before having my IUD inserted, I took a pregnancy test. When the timer went off, the nurse looked at the test and told me she'd be right back. From the awkward tone in her voice, I knew I was pregnant. I also knew I was going to have an abortion.

My mom was waiting outside the office to take me home. She asked how my IUD insertion went and I handed her the piece of paper I'd been given with the abortion clinic's referral information. She held me in the lobby as I cried. Later that night, she came into my bedroom with a bag full of candy and told me everything was going to be okay. I've always believed in the right to choose, but I never thought I'd find myself in that situation as a kid.

I'VE ALWAYS BELIEVED IN THE RIGHT TO CHOOSE, BUT I NEVER THOUGHT I'D FIND MYSELF IN THAT SITUATION AS A KID.

I scheduled my abortion a few days later for a Friday morning. That morning, I woke up very early several times in order to take the medication I was prescribed to make the procedure as comfortable as possible. Instead of taking the bus to school, I took the bus to Group Health with my then-boyfriend, who was very supportive.

After getting all checked in, my boyfriend and I got ourselves settled in the room. They allowed him to stay with me during the entire procedure. He held my hand the whole time and even rubbed my tummy when I jokingly asked him to. My abortion took all of 15 minutes, which also included finally getting that IUD inserted after the procedure was over.

The abortion was physically and emotionally painless for me. I was so well taken care of by the nurses, the doctors, and my loved ones that my visit was nothing more than just a regular doctor's visit. After walking out into the waiting room, my mom gave me a big hug and a donut and took us home. I proceeded to have the best nap of my life, followed by the best meal of my life, because the pregnancy had been making me ill and it was gone.

I spent the next few days with friends and classmates feeling like I was keeping a huge secret—like they didn't truly know me because they didn't know I'd just had an abortion. So I decided I wanted to make an announcement to my senior class. I'd told my best friend about what was going on and why I wanted to share it with everyone, and she could not have been more supportive and encouraging. I'm so thankful for her.

A week later, during the "weekend share" segment of class, I stood up and started talking, immediately feeling discouraged because no one was really paying attention. Then I said the words "I had an abortion," and everyone froze and looked up. There was a moment of silence followed by a short round of applause—which I appreciated, but it wasn't the response I needed. I just wanted someone to show me compassion and acknowledge the weight of my disclosure. After that, I called a meeting with my classmates to discuss how we hold space for other people. In that meeting and afterward I felt I received the acknowledgment and respect I was hoping for.

Abortion stigma has the power to consume people, some with debilitating shame and others with hatred. I've always known that my abortion experience was somewhat of a privilege: I had unconditional love and support from my family and friends, and I didn't feel guilty about my decision. My gratitude motivated me to continue discussing my experience with others, because I believe that honest conversations about abortion can help people become less judgmental and potentially more supportive of the people around them. I dedicated my yearlong senior project to the topic of abortion stigma, exploring the ways that stigma—not abortion—is often a deep source of trauma.

Nothing has empowered me like sharing my abortion story with the world. It has defined me in a way I wouldn't trade for anything, and Shout Your Abortion has been a huge part of that. SYA helped me understand that abortion is normal, helped me trust that my abortion was the right choice for me, and empowered me to share my story openly. SYA made me know I never have to be ashamed.

I never knew that just talking about my own abortion experience would be so impactful, but now I do, and I'm never going to stop. ■

OUR RIGHTS ARE NON-NEGOTIABLE
SAFE ABORTIONS SAVE LIVES

AMY JOCHSETT

Anyone who opposes abortion access should know what it's like to have an illegal abortion. They should know that criminalizing abortion doesn't stop people from having them; it only makes it more dangerous.

I grew up in Mexico, where abortion is illegal and very stigmatized. When I was 16, I was sexually assaulted by a family member and became pregnant. My body became numb when the nurse told me I was pregnant; it just didn't feel real. I didn't know what to do or who to talk to. All I wanted was to finish high school and get a college degree, but most importantly, I didn't want to have a child from my rapist.

I KNEW ABORTION WASN'T LEGAL BUT THAT DIDN'T STOP ME.

I knew abortion wasn't legal but that didn't stop me.

I searched the internet and found an unlicensed provider who was willing to help me. I did anything I could to raise the money for my procedure. I sang in buses and cleaned people's houses for almost three weeks.

On the day of the procedure, the provider asked me if I wanted to call someone before he began: "You may wanna call someone just in case you don't wake up." I called my grandma to tell her how much I loved her. I was terrified, but I decided to have the procedure anyway.

Although I was sedated, I ended up waking up toward the end of the procedure. It felt like my insides were burning, I thought I wasn't going to make it. After everything was done I went home to recover alone.

Later that night I was taken to the emergency room by a neighbor due to a severe uterine infection with a high fever and a hemorrhage. The abortion was dangerous, and I nearly died because it had to be done secretly, without the proper safety precautions. After my recovery, I decided to move to the U.S. to finish my education.

Shortly after moving, I learned that Wisconsin has one of the toughest abortion laws in the country, so I decided to start volunteering at Planned Parenthood with my friends. I wasn't familiar with Planned Parenthood at the time, but I knew I wanted to be an advocate for reproductive justice.

With time, I became more comfortable talking about abortion, but for some reason I still didn't feel confident enough to tell my own story. Shout Your Abortion helped me realize that I am not alone, that abortion is normal, and that I have nothing to be ashamed of. Reading the stories of all those women made me feel stronger and empowered, and allowed me to heal. Suddenly, I wasn't afraid anymore. I want to share my story so that people understand the dangers of restricting abortion access. I don't want anyone else to ever go through what I've gone through. ■

EL SANCHEZ

"El, my period is late."

I froze in place for a moment, clutching my cell phone in silence before slowly melting into a nearby chair. "How late?" I asked. "Like, almost two months," Michelle answered, with the upturned tone and cadence of a question rather than an answer. Michelle (not her real name) was my best friend since freshman year of high school. Just a few months earlier I had moved to Seattle from our small hometown in Washington State following the failure of an early and unnecessary marriage. Michelle had moved from the house she had shared with myself and my then spouse to Seattle a year earlier to attend art school. I was excited to put some distance between myself and the emotional responsibilities of my first divorce, as well as some much-needed distance between myself and my MANY embarrassingly sloppy drunk post-separation hookups in my hometown. Unfortunately, Michelle and I only had a month or so to reconnect before she had "fallen in love" with some creep she met from a Missed Connection on Craigslist. I'll call him Dave because that's pretty close to his actual boring-ass name. Between their many breakups and makeups, we barely had time to mourn my personal heartbreak.

"El, I don't know what to do, "she sobbed, "I'm scared." The truth was, I didn't know what to do either, but that's not what you tell your best friend. Instead, I came up with a plan. "Let's both go buy a pregnancy test right now. Then we can take them at the same time and call each other with the results." I thought the camaraderie of simultaneously taking a test would help her to feel less embarrassed and alone, plus my own period was three days late. I could not only be a supportive friend, but also give myself peace of mind in the process. She agreed to this plan and we both hung up the phone. I hurried to the grocery store, purchased the test and a pack of cigarettes, then smoked a fresh one on the walk back to my apartment. Once inside, I opened a PBR which I sipped to calm my nerves and help me pee. I unwrapped the stick, peed on the end, placed it on the edge of the sink, and waited. I wasn't worried for myself, but I felt anxious for Michelle. It was very likely she was pregnant. I wondered whether she would keep the baby as a terrible attempt to keep Dave in her life. The alarm I had set on my phone sounded. I sat on the edge of my bathtub, holding my phone tight as I prepared for Michelle's inevitable phone call and grabbed the stick off of the edge of my sink. I glanced at it as my phone began ringing. I held my breath as I pressed the answer button. "El??" her voice cracked through sobs, "I'm pregnant." I paused for a moment. "Me too," I replied.

HOW HAD THIS HAPPENED? I screamed over and over in my head. Truthfully, I knew. I had been having sex with a cis dude and hadn't been using condoms. I mean, we did sometimes, but there were also times I would drunkenly rip them off and whisper something I thought sounded sexy in his ear like, "I hope I don't regret this," which, as I write this, I realize isn't sexy at all (and I also realize I'm writing "drunken" as a description far too often). In addition to my lack of experience with (what I assume straights refer to as) "getting goofed in," I wasn't on birth control because I was too lazy to have my prescription forwarded to a pharmacy in Seattle and had decided the pills were unnecessary since most of my sexual partners post divorce did not have penises. Michelle wasn't sure what to do, but I was positive. No question, I was having an abortion.

It felt odd making that decision, as I had always been pro-choice politically, but had never been in the position where I actually needed to make that choice. I knew I wasn't ready for the responsibility of a child. The dude I'd been sleeping with for two weeks was one of the part-time managers at a theater I worked, and he had a girlfriend he planned on getting back together with once she graduated from college in New York. Nothing about my life seemed appropriate for a child. The only decision left to make was if I should I tell him, but that decision was made by my mother when I called her to tell her the news. "You're going to tell him, right?" she asked. "I'm not sure," I replied. "I don't really want to deal with any weirdness."

"El," my mother said sternly, "you absolutely have to tell him. He has the right to know. Plus, he needs to pay for it."

I agonized over the best way to do it. Should I seem emotional or levelheaded? Would a lack of emotion cause him to think I lacked human empathy? OR, would acting emotional make me seem like I was overreacting? Scott (his fake name) came over later that night and everything went as planned. Beers, bad movies, boning, the usual. Only this time, I requested he goof in me. He obliged. Afterward, he breathily commented, "We probably shouldn't do that, you could get pregnant." I calmly turned over on the mattress pad that I had stuffed into a walk-in closet in my studio apartment, making it my makeshift bedroom. "No worries. I'm already pregnant," I said, feeling positive I had chosen the best way possible to share this news. After an hour of hyperventilating and asking uncomfortable questions, Scott requested to go to the clinic with me. So we made a date, our very first date in the daytime.

AS THE PROCEDURE BEGINS, THEY TELL HIM HE CAN HOLD MY HAND. WE LOOK AT EACH OTHER AND REALIZE WE HAVEN'T HELD HANDS BEFORE.

Michelle eventually decided she would terminate as well so I scheduled our appointments on the same day to support her. Unfortunately, Dave was there too and moved their appointment earlier in the morning to avoid me. The morning of the procedure, I wore the required baggy pants and shirt, picked up some coffee from Starbucks, and went with Scott to Planned Parenthood. My first observation in the waiting room was the amount of women there who were also in baggy clothes and holding coffee cups. I wished we could acknowledge each other with some kind of wink or nod, but reminded myself everyone's experience was different and my "day at the office" attitude about this could feel fucked up to some people. Plus, for all I knew, they were just there for annual paps. I turned my attention to the television, which was playing an episode of *The Bonnie Hunt Show*. I had no idea that was a thing.

Finally. They called me back and I knew it was almost time for the procedure. Scott said he'd see me "back there" and we awkwardly laughed for some reason. In my gown in the room with my feet in the straps, I was struck by how casual the whole thing is. We were basically in an average exam room. There were no bells and whistles, just a machine, one doctor, and one nurse's aide. They asked me if I wanted Scott in the room. I said sure.

As the procedure begins, they tell him he can hold my hand. We look at each other and realize we haven't held hands before. During the procedure his chair faces the wall behind my head. As he holds my hand with my legs up in the air, it's almost like I'm giving birth and he's there to cheer me on. Behind my head on the wall is a giant diagram of a penis. It's oddly quiet. I decide to break the ice. "Hey Scott," I ask. "What are you up to?" "Oh, just looking at a diagram of a dick," he replies. "How about you?" "Meh, not much, just having an abortion," I reply. The nurse laughs, then muffles her mouth. The doctor cracks a smile then shakes it off. She seems disappointed in herself and tries to make small talk with me. Knowing I work at a movie theater she says, "So, El, are there any good movies playing right now?" I can barely hear her soft voice over the sound of the machine. "Dr. Kyle, I really want to answer your question, but I'm kind of in the middle of an abortion right now…" I respond. The doctor cracks a smile again and almost lets a laugh slip. I tell myself I'm going to make her laugh before I leave.

When it's over, I'm lying in a comfy chair in the Recovery Room where your abdomen is covered in heating pads and nurses ply you with crackers and soda. I request as many snacks as possible to hoard for later. I know I'm not going to want to walk to the store later, plus I love free stuff. I see a small group of women crying together in a corner of the recovery room, and two of them are chewing on granola bars. A nurse walks by and I grab her attention. "Excuse me?" I ask, "Can I get a couple granola bars?" She pulls out various things from cupboards nearby and does not look at me. "We don't have granola bars," she says, still avoiding eye contact. She leaves the room.

A few moments later, my doctor enters the room. She nods in support at the crying women and then walks over to me. "Well, El, you're all ready to go. Is there anything else you need?" she asks. "Yes, actually," I reply. "Can I have a granola bar?" The doctor stares up at the ceiling before repeating the same lie as the previous nurse. My painkillers are wearing off and I don't have time for bullshit. "Listen," I reply quietly, gesturing for the doctor to lean in. "Do I have to cry to get some Nature Valley in here, because I WILL." Doctor Kyle looks shocked for a second before letting out an audible laugh. I feel victorious. She brings me some granola bars. As I stand up to leave, Dr. Kyle walks over to me with a bouquet of flowers in a glass vase. "I want to present you with these flowers. We always give flowers to the final patient of the day." I look around the recovery room, and the three women are still there. "But I'm not the last patient," I respond, confused. Dr. Kyle leans in close to me and whispers in my ear, "I know you're not the last patient, but you're getting these flowers because you're the funniest abortion I've ever performed." She hands me the flowers, and the story of the greatest achievement of my comedy career.

It's been eight years since that day. I went on to marry Scott a few years later, only to divorce him some years after that. I had a second abortion a couple years ago, which ended up being less funny—both on my end and the experience itself. I came out as trans non-binary two years ago, which has helped put so much of my life into perspective. Also, three weeks prior to writing this piece, I had my first child. I have since found out that abortions are not similar to giving birth. Abortions are much easier. I am extremely glad I had both of mine when I did.

Four months after my first abortion, I performed at my very first open mic, having been somewhat encouraged by Dr. Kyle. Four years later, hours after my second abortion, I performed a standup set that night, as well as a musical performance as a member of my Michael Bolton cover band Lightning Bolton, where I managed to do my patented stage-dive/knee-slide at the climax of "How Can We Be Lovers" despite the cramps. I've gone on to have a semi-successful comedy career, something that was a dream I've had since I was a little kid, and something I never would've achieved if I hadn't had that abortion. In fact, now that I think about it, it's something that may end now that I have a child. Damn it. ■

JESSA JORDAN

When I was 21, my budding baby-anarchist/art-hoe lifestyle was more exciting, more financially viable—and somehow even more sustainable—than the prospect of sitting through another three-hour lecture on Shakespeare, or raising money for the undergraduate literature and art magazine I managed. I was able to strip and go-go dance in any dive bar that would have me, and I took full advantage of the newfound fame brought my way thanks to some professionally executed nudes reblogged blowing up on Tumblr.

Bambi-eyed, baby-faced, and just buxom enough, I threw myself to the wolves, insisting that I be taken seriously as a proud pro-hoe. In fact, when my images circulated enough that people began recognizing me offline, some of my peers thought it appropriate to label me "the porn star" because of my extracurriculars. For the first time ever, I was drunk on a strange power. I was in control of my body, my sexuality, and my life, and I didn't want to stop until I was Kim K. famous. I wanted nothing more than to be the best "slut" I could be—the smartass who could talk your ear off about Nietzsche or Nabokov and get paid generously for every grin and growl I offered. While I was still a few years away from choosing to work as an escort, I was beginning to be much more selective in the partners I chose for sex anyway.

CARRYING OUT AN UNPLANNED AND UNWANTED PREGNANCY WOULD HAVE BEEN DEVASTATING TO ME PHYSICALLY, FINANCIALLY, AND EMOTIONALLY.

My sexual appetite was changing primarily because I was finding out how exhausting cis-het men were. While I still wanted to fuck often—and did if it wasn't near midterms or finals weeks—I didn't want to fuck the same guys who'd wanted to use me solely as the vessel for their pleasure and dismissed the thought of reciprocating. Even worse was the thought that I was undeserving of love and intimacy because I was just another nameless slut they could easily coax back to their bedroom. It was a strange and fascinating concept to reconcile: I could be desired and fucked, but not also loved, at least not by guys who didn't think I was worthy of love or commitment because I was just so slutty.

Unsurprisingly, the night of conception was far from immaculate. I was supporting my then-dormmate Khadija in her attempt to break into the competitive Philadelphia nightlife scene as a DJ. We went to a party on a balmy Saturday night in May 2012 at a local anarchist meeting room known affectionately as the A-Space. I got drunk and danced around with other local Philly queers and punks, trying to release all my stress and life's annoyances. And then it happened. I saw and overheard a cis-male screaming in the face of a fellow femme. I moved in between them, immediately stopping him in his tracks, surprising and further angering him that another woman would step to him. I didn't give a shit; I wasn't going to let any man abuse a woman in my presence. Before I had to exert any more effort, people came to our aid and the aggressor was removed from the venue. Apparently he had a long history of abusing women, abusing power, and abusing the bodies of anyone who brought up the former. I was warned to be careful as Khadija and I made our way back to our dorm, but it made no difference. The fight had ruined my buzz and I needed to calm the live wires that were my veins. So I called Alex up since I knew he was the only dude I could reach out to who would be awake, DTF, and willing to travel to me at 4:00 a.m.

Since Khadija was asleep when Alex arrived, we stayed in the living room and ended up fucking on the floor atop a haphazardly placed pile of blankets and pillows. I didn't enjoy it, and that was amplified by the annoyance I felt once I realized the condom that had been there at the beginning had become a casualty along the way. I didn't find it in the blankets. I didn't find it on the floor. To this day, I can't tell you where it went, but I can say the immediate horror I felt at the realization. This person—basically a fucking stranger—had just ejaculated inside of me. I was floored. In all my whorish history I had never experienced this. I didn't know how to handle it, so I just went to sleep.

We talked about it the next morning awkwardly outside my building while he unlocked his bicycle. I don't remember if he offered to pay for the Plan B I was preparing to buy the next day, but he was confident he didn't have any STDs, which was mildly comforting. Once I took the Plan B and confirmed I was negative for all major STIs, worrying about those sorts of issues became a bad memory.

A short few weeks later, I showed up at Thomas Jefferson University Hospital exhibiting every symptom of a panic attack—though I was convinced it was a stroke or heart attack since those had ended various lives in my family. After multiple CAT scans, the verdict was official: I was physically fine and definitely pregnant.

I was early enough along to have a medication abortion. From that moment on, I chose survival over everything. Survival through the guilt that was wreaking havoc on my psyche for "slutting it up" so much, and not being more aware of what was happening, to me and inside of me. Survival through the societal pressure to be a perfect student, a perfect young woman, and a perfect whore—smart enough to make the decision to fuck on my own, but avoid the crossfire of consequences. Survival through the men I'd been sleeping with and their desire to destroy any self-love or peace of mind I kept for myself.

Looking back on it, I know that I made the right choice for my one wild life. I feel empowered by having the strength to persevere, instead of carrying out an unplanned and unwanted pregnancy, which would have been devastating to me physically, financially, and emotionally. Instead, I could pursue a life free of draining, toxic lovers and raise my spirit—weaponizing my own existence as the whore, the Madonna, and everything infinite in between.

In everyday conversations, I hear people discuss survival. No one has ever said to me that choosing to have an abortion is an act of survival, but I know now that it is. ■

CHAPEL OF PRAYER
A.D.
MCMLVI
EVERYONE KNOWS I HAD AN ABORTION

KEEP ABORTION LEGAL
PRO-CHOICE
CLINIC ESCORT

LAUREL

In the spring of 2014, my boyfriend and I decided that I would stop taking birth control. That June, I started a new job in Galveston, Texas—a town about an hour away from my home, boyfriend, family, and friends. I attempted the commute for a couple of weeks before realizing it was not feasible for the long term and deciding to move. By this point, I had come to realize that the timing was not good for a pregnancy. In addition to leaving my entire support system, I had taken a pay cut in my new position. But I'd always heard that it would be at least six months to a year before I would get pregnant after being on birth control for so long.

I'M SO GRATEFUL THAT I DON'T HAVE TO TRY TO COPARENT A CHILD WITH THAT PERSON FOR THE REST OF OUR LIVES.

On the morning that I was scheduled to move, I opened the tote that held my gardening supplies and immediately fled to the bathroom to be ill. I called my sister, who told me to go get a test. I called her back, weeping, when it was positive. After taking a few days to myself to process, I told my boyfriend. He was wholly unsupportive. He had a daughter from his previous marriage and said he still had things he wanted to do in his life, bills of his own to pay, and that he wasn't ready for another child. I was flabbergasted. We had mutually agreed to try to conceive—why did he agree to this if he was going to be upset when I actually got pregnant? He said he thought that "conceiving" meant we would be intimate more often, which made no sense to me.

I Googled "abortion in Houston" and set up a consultation appointment. In Texas, there is a mandatory 24-hour waiting period, meaning the abortion consists of two appointments with a 24-hour waiting period in between. The consultation was August 26, and the abortion was scheduled for the day after, which happened to be my 28th birthday. During the counseling portion of the first appointment I broke down in tears, and the counselor recommended I take a few days to make a final decision. After going home and talking it over with my parents, I knew abortion was the only logical choice to make. My parents drove me back to the clinic that Saturday; alongside the Clinic Defense Team, they helped shield me from the protesters.

It was more than a year later before I stopped feeling guilty for terminating a pregnancy that I thought I wanted. But I know today, even more than I did then, that it was the right thing for me to do. After my abortion, my boyfriend and I split up and I'm so grateful that I don't have to try to coparent a child with that person for the rest of our lives. He would have resented me if I kept the pregnancy, and he also would have resented our child. After the abortion, I accepted a better job back in my home county. I've since been promoted and have started traveling with my parents. None of these things would be possible if I were a single parent with a small child in tow.

A couple of years after my abortion, I found myself wanting to give back through some kind of volunteer work. I remembered the kind individuals who ushered me into the clinic that day, defending me from the abusive protesters and helping me get inside safely. I contacted the organization that handles the Clinic Defense Team at the same clinic where I had my abortion, and I have now been volunteering with the team for nearly a year. On every shift, I hope to make someone else's difficult situation just a little easier by offering them care and respect, and I'm glad my own abortion has allowed me to find such a meaningful way to support others who are making the same choice. ■

ALAYNA BECKER

In 1915, my great-great-grandmother, Iva Urie, had an illegal abortion arranged by her second husband, Archie. Iva was already a loving mother to Floyd, her 11-year-old son from her first marriage. Archie didn't want another child.

Floyd, my great-grandfather, was sent out of the house during the abortion. His options were limited: he could chop wood or go into town to watch the brawls that regularly spilled out of Mountain View, Washington's one tavern. Floyd chose the fights. He watched as two men, one missing an arm from a logging accident, barreled out of the tavern and tangled up in the muddy road. He watched as they beat each other bloody, blood churning into the muddy ground until it disappeared. Floyd, my great-grandfather, had no idea what was going on at home.

I had my first abortion at 17, at the home of my boyfriend's parents. I chose a medical abortion. I took two small, white pills over the course of two days and cramped out the pregnancy in the living room. I threw up while watching *16 and Pregnant* on MTV while my boyfriend's mom rubbed my back. I snacked on apples and peanut butter. I cried, missing my own mother. I made 30 trips to the bathroom that night, watching as clumps of clotted blood swirled in the toilet. I was too young, too unstable, too focused; too much and simultaneously not enough to become a mother.

THE WOMEN IN MY FAMILY ARE THE SECRET HOLDERS.

Iva's abortion went badly. She bled onto the sheets of newspaper covering her thin mattress, which sat directly on the springs of her iron bed frame inside the cheap cedar walls of a home that was never built to last—just one tiny room for the three of them. I think about the pale floral curtains she hung around the tiny, wavy glass windows, the kind of windows that make the rest of the world look distorted.

Three years before Iva's abortion, she had run away from her abusive first husband, my great-great-grandfather William, in Rochester, New York. The night she ran, there had been a fight, and William wouldn't let go of Floyd. Iva picked up a dinner plate from the table and smashed it over William's head, freeing Floyd from his grip. Iva and Floyd left that night. Floyd stayed in an orphanage until Iva could find a job and feed him again, then picked him up and moved the two of them across the country to Portland, Oregon, hoping for a better life where they could finally live free of William's fists.

On the day of her abortion, an unskilled midwife from town had attempted to sanitize improvised abortion instruments in water on the stove. The hot water boiled over the walls of the pot onto the wood stove, sizzling into puddles before disappearing. The midwife pulled the foot-long wire she planned to use to end the pregnancy into the air. She then pushed the wire into Iva's uterus without the guidance of even a speculum or a light. Without pain medication or antibiotics, Iva screamed and thrashed. She began to bleed uncontrollably. Twenty miles from any medical care, she died in her home at the age of 28. Iva's death certificate says she was buried with an unnamed infant.

When Floyd returned home that night, Archie told him that his mother died of a hemorrhage, handed him a five-dollar bill and a note that said "good luck," and took off into the night. Floyd lived his life believing that his mother had died as the result of a freak accident, not from a heinous lack of rights and medical care. Nobody ever told him the truth.

My last abortion was performed in a Planned Parenthood by a physician. I was fortunate enough to afford anesthesia—which, even to this day, is considered a luxury, only offered to women with insurance or who are able to pay. I went under while Lionel Richie's "All Night Long" played on the boombox in the exam room. When I woke up, the procedure was over, and the chorus was still playing: "Fiesta, Forever." "All Night Long" lasts four minutes and 19 seconds. I went home to eat mac and cheese with a heating pad my boyfriend bought me. I ruined another mattress by way of a leaky maxi pad. The next day, I went to work.

The only person who was told the truth about the abortion was Iva's sister, who told my grandmother, who told me. The women in my family are the secret holders. They are the quiet battleaxes. They kept Iva's truth a secret from Floyd to protect him. But lies don't protect victims, they protect the perpetrators. Lies protected Archie. Lies have protected twisted lawmakers, who have regulated women's healthcare in a way that subjects people to brutal mistakes, making abortion an institutional bloodsport.

Floyd was an orphan who spent his life missing his mother. He would go on to marry another orphan, melding their two broken hearts and trying to create what they didn't have, but parents can only learn to love the lives they create by being loved. The trauma of abandonment lives in our familial bloodline. Lost and looking is in my DNA. It lives in tall glasses of wine, it lives in our depressed brains, it lives in our hands steadying ourselves against messy lovers. Generation by generation, the reverberation of Iva's death is felt in our bones, like a ripple—barely detectable but infinite. ■

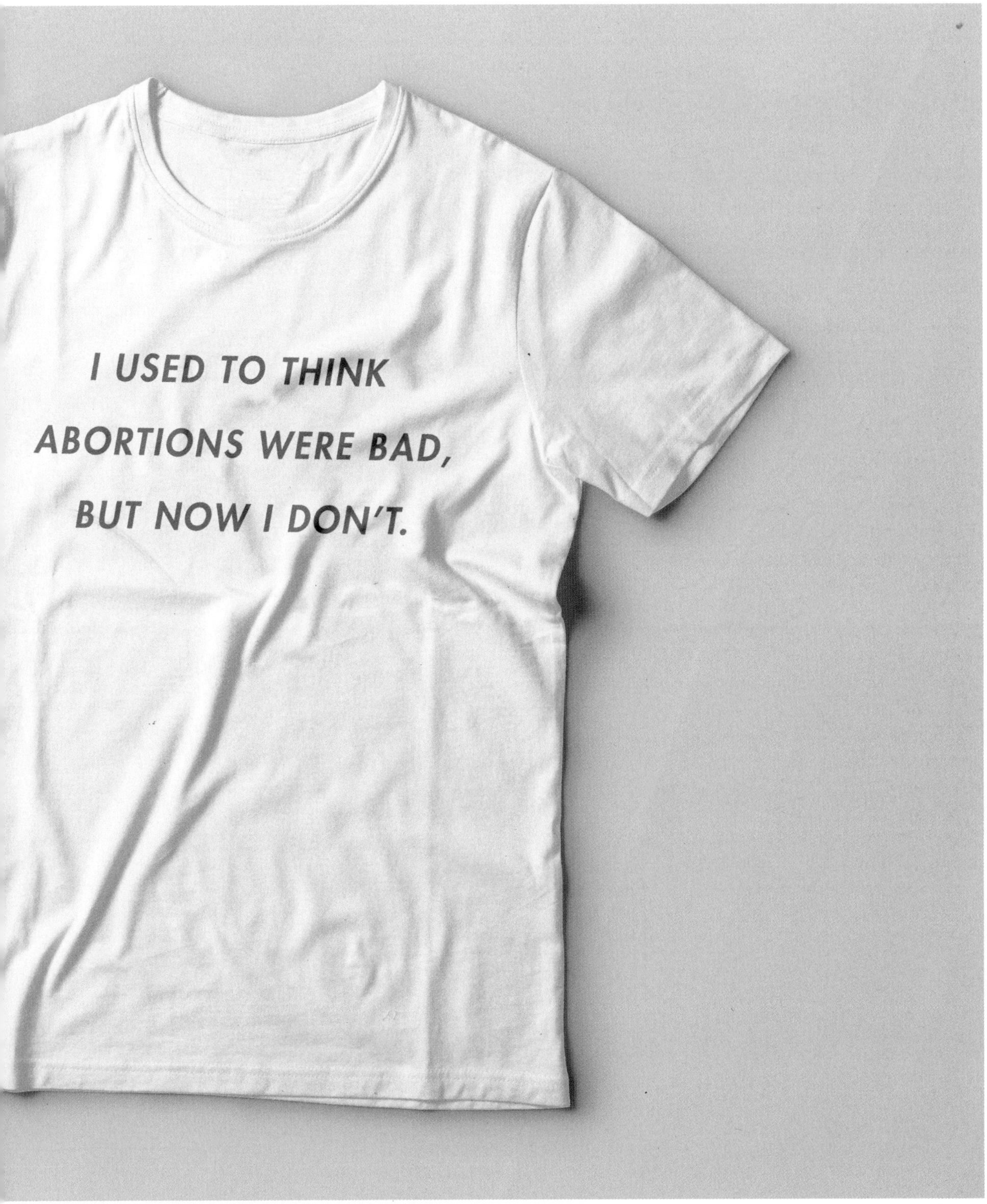

I USED TO THINK
ABORTIONS WERE BAD,
BUT NOW I DON'T.

ALANA EDMONDSON

I found out I was pregnant in February 2010, only four months after my 21st birthday. I had been dating my boyfriend, who was nine years my elder, for approximately two months. We'd had our first date on Christmas after meeting at a bar a week or two prior. I'd suspected that I might be pregnant for some time, but I'd been unable to take a test and face my reality. At the time, I was still in the process of letting go of my faith in Christianity and recognizing the effects Christianity had on my daily thinking. I was no longer Christian and no longer believed in any God, but my first two visceral responses to my pregnancy were the paradoxical "No" and "I don't want to kill anyone." First, I did not want to subscribe to the "If my mama can do it, I can do it" mentality. I knew that motherhood was a choice I was neither ready nor required to undertake. I also felt that to have an abortion would mean that I had singlehandedly denied someone the right to live. But ultimately I didn't believe aborting a fetus was the same as ending a human life.

I WAS A WOMAN SECURE WITH MYSELF AND MY SEXUALITY, ACTIVELY MAKING CHOICES AND TAKING ACTION TOWARD THE FUTURE.

A family friend sent me to a clinic that was ambiguously described as a place that could assist me in choosing an option. This "clinic," however, did nothing of the sort. The tables in the lobby held magazines promoting adoption and even included profiles of families looking to adopt. As I spoke with a counselor, I quickly realized their sole objective was talking me out of having an abortion when I thought I had come to discuss all my options. I left that fake clinic (also known as a "crisis pregnancy center") with an ultrasound photo of the embryo, newborn booties, and a baby blanket. My confusion was palpable. I named the alien inside of me "Feet"—he started as "Fetus"—and spoke to him often.

I didn't get an abortion until I was 11 weeks pregnant. This is because I did so much research beforehand, because I spent so much time speaking with the women in my life, mothers I knew, friends, and siblings. I considered adoption, and my older sister even offered to raise the baby as part of her family. During the five weeks I knew I was pregnant, I learned something about myself: if I gave birth to a child, I wouldn't want to give it away. I would keep it. Termination became the only option.

The night before the procedure, I sobbed on my couch, rocking back and forth. I clutched my bloated belly and cried to Feet, "I'm so sorry, I'm so sorry." My boyfriend and I went to Planned Parenthood early the next morning, and I was calm. I was doing the right thing. I requested a final ultrasound so that I could say goodbye to Feet. He had grown three times bigger than the last time I had seen him at the covert anti-choice clinic I'd visited only weeks before. The speed of his growth terrified me. I quickly said goodbye to Feet and hastily swallowed the medicine provided to soften my cervix and my nerves. The medical staff was comforting and professional. I felt little to no pain, and I left Planned Parenthood feeling gloriously empty, magnificently grateful that I lived in a place and had the means to take control over my body, my life, and my future.

Years later, I was living in Seattle when Shout Your Abortion exploded. At the time, I was working on embracing things that frightened me, and shouting my abortion definitely fit the bill, so I volunteered to tell my story on camera for SYA's new YouTube channel. It was incredibly empowering to openly discuss my choice and to take my first leap into shattering the way I've been socialized to treat abortion as too taboo to be discussed.

My involvement with SYA eventually led to my participation in a national marketing campaign with Planned Parenthood, which has been one of the most rewarding things I have ever been a part of—the video ad in particular. The bar where I work is called Witness, and twice a week staff members offer "sermons" to whoever happens to be sitting in the bar. Sermons cover a range of topics, generally beginning with something anecdotal and ending with a call to recognize or attempt certain behaviors that week. I've given sermons on doing my first movie for an erotic film festival ("Try something that scares you!"), on dating in Seattle ("Stop ghosting and give more cunnilingus!"), and on my fear of being the "angry black woman" stereotype ("I'm allowed to be angry in response to routine injustice and so are you!").

I STILL REALLY BELIEVE IN DOING THINGS THAT SCARE ME AS A WAY TO NEUTRALIZE MY OWN SENSE OF FEAR, AND I KEEP GETTING BRAVER.

In collaboration with the Planned Parenthood marketing campaign, I gave a sermon about my abortion. I spoke to a packed bar of people on first dates, celebrating birthdays and anniversaries, and enjoying a casual cocktail with friends, many of whom did not anticipate hearing a sermon in a bar, let alone about abortion. I literally shouted my abortion to 60 strangers, friends, and coworkers, on video. It was one of the most nerve-racking experiences of my life, and when it was all said and done I felt super brave. I also felt certain that my sermon had sparked a lot of conversations that wouldn't have happened otherwise and maybe helped a few people who'd had abortions realize that silence and shame are not the only option.

In July 2017, I learned that I was pregnant again with my partner of only one month. This time, I was not the 21-year-old girl I was before. I was 28, a woman secure with myself and my sexuality, actively making choices and taking action toward the future I envisioned for myself. My partner and I knew we wanted to have children together someday but ultimately decided we wanted more time to establish a stronger foundation in our relationship. This pregnancy was infinitely more painful than my first, in the sense that I wanted to let this embryo grow so that I could love and raise it with my partner. I felt ready for motherhood, but the timing just wasn't right. So I had another abortion, this time with my partner in the room holding my hand as hot tears streamed down my face. This abortion was so much different yet still the same; while the procedure was remarkably painful both physically and emotionally, I left Planned Parenthood feeling the same overwhelming sense of gratitude as I had leaving that same building seven years earlier.

I had my abortion at 8:15 a.m., and at 4:00 p.m. that same day I was scheduled to speak at a rally. The Seattle Storm had become the first professional sports team to publicly endorse Planned Parenthood, and I'd been asked to speak on behalf of PP patients. I announced to the crowd of hundreds that I'd had an abortion only hours prior to standing at that podium to address them. I shouted to WNBA players and reporters, to mothers and daughters, and to the 30 anti-choice protesters holding enlarged posters of aborted fetuses and signs reading "ABORTION IS MURDER." It felt fucking amazing.

I still really believe in doing things that scare me as a way to neutralize my own sense of fear, and I keep getting braver. The louder I shout, the more I know I'm helping other people do the same. ■

SYA
MY CHOICE
MY FREEDOM
NO REGRETS

POPPY LIU

Story by Poppy Liu and her mother, as adapted from Poppy's film Names of Women.
Design and illustration by Zoraida Ingles

In order to tell my abortion story I have to begin with my mother, immigrating from China to America in 1993.

Because I cannot tell my abortion story without telling my family's stories.

My abortion story is the migration of my parents. It is this queer yellow body; Chenglish as a language of choice.

It is lineages of people I come from who believe in endurance and sacrifice so that the next generation can "have it better."

I have to start telling my story from here.

Immediately after I found out I was pregnant I audio recorded myself.

There are some days when I feel more human than others.

And I felt very human that day.

The day after I found out I was pregnant was the day of the blood super moon.

That night, under the moon, holding the hands of two women I love, I cried but I did not tell either of them that I was pregnant.

I remembered that I am made of stardust; stars made me.

I finally felt pregnant, which is strange to say because...

I feel pregnant all the time.

I feel like a mother all the time. My whole body feels like a womb.

I didn't feel any shame or guilt. I knew what I had to do, but I did feel pregnant.

Today what I remember from all of this is the women:

Eleanor and Nicole and Ruth, the nurses.

Tash, Tania, Ellen, Kate, and the 13 women who put their 26 hands on my body and told me to let go.

My sister Zoe, age 6, who says "I'm not afraid of anything."

Leah, my mother, who taught me that we have inner worlds greater than we have words for.

One year after my abortion, I went public with my story and finally told my mother. I waited at home for her to call me from China and finally she did. When I picked up the video call and we saw each other on our cell phone screens we both started crying.

She kept saying, "I will always hold you" over and over again.

And then she told me her abortion story, which I didn't know until that day.

I had a dream the night after my abortion. I dreamed of a swan outside my house. It kept pounding on the window with its beak. It wanted to come in but it couldn't. On the window, pounding and pounding, until finally it flew away.

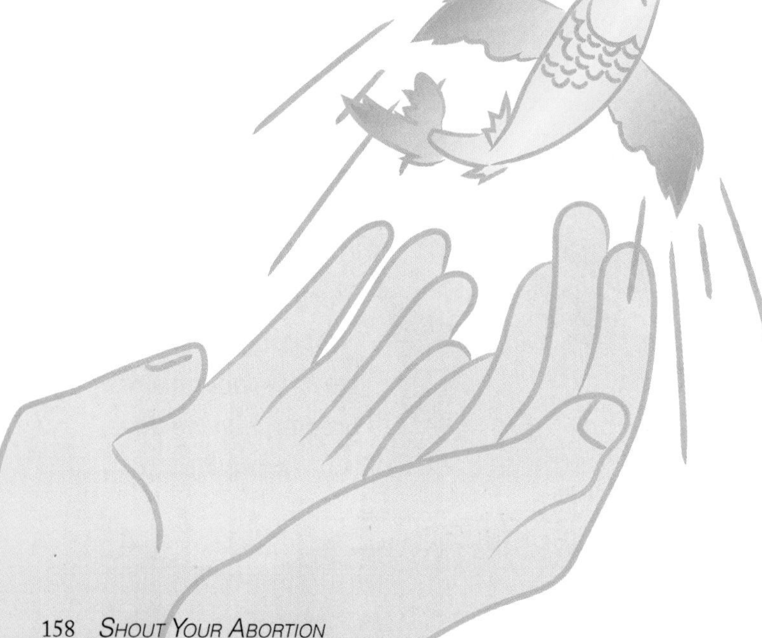

Later that night, I had another dream. I was clutching something in my hand. When I opened it, I saw a fish covered in gold. It was flopping around "pata pata patapata"—faster and faster until it also flew away. When I woke up I knew that was the baby.

After my second miscarriage I couldn't get out of bed. I bled so much, I was completely pale, and my lips were peeling off.

You were 5 then. I remember you looked at me and said, "Mom, why do you want another baby?" You didn't understand.

I said, "Child, isn't it because I want to give you a sibling?"

I thought you would say, "Thank you mama, you did this all for us!" So I was looking at you eagerly and guess what you said?

You just said, "Uh oh." You even shrugged your shoulders "Uh oh." You said, "Don't you see? This is your life, your own life. You should do this for you, not for me."

You know I was suddenly shaken awake at that moment.

When you told me about your abortion, my heart was hurting so much. Because I wasn't there with you after the abortion. I wasn't there with you for "the little month."

I didn't tell you anything and you were just out there trying and walking this path by yourself.

You know, your grandma still doesn't know about my abortion.

When you said, "I will always hold you," after I told you about my abortion, I felt myself heal in a way that I didn't even know I needed.

I realized in that moment that in our inheritance we don't just pass down joy.

We also pass down pain, we pass down silence, and we pass down shame.

But all it takes is one generation, one link, to reverse this.

Turn those silences into words that we can say. Turn that pain into love.

THE STORY OF MY ABORTION
BY TATIANA GILL
FROM PUBERTY ON, MY BIGGEST FEAR WAS GETTING PREGNANT.
MY PERIOD WAS NEVER REGULAR. I WASN'T EVEN HAVING SEX YET, BUT...
WHEN I WAS 16 I DID A LITTLE 'HEAVY PETTING' AND DIDN'T GET MY PERIOD FOR MONTHS AFTER.
PLEASE GOD*
STILL NOTHING
DON'T LET ME BE PREGNANT
*DIDN'T BELEIVE IN GOD -WAS PRAYING ANYWAYS!
I FELT TRAPPED. EVEN WITH LIBERAL PARENTS THERE WAS NO WAY I WAS MENTIONING IT TO THEM.
$20!!! I DON'T HAVE $20!
EPT
PREGNANCY TEST-$20
OTHER TEST-$40
THANKFULLY A FRIEND TOLD ME TO TRY PLANNED PARENTHOOD
YOUR TEST SHOWS YOU'RE NOT PREGNANT
AND, THERE'S NO CHARGE
THANK YOU!
OVER THE NEXT DOZEN YEARS I HAD OTHER SCARES. MANY EPT'S WERE USED. MY PERIOD STILL ONLY SHOWED UP A FEW TIMES A YEAR.
not pregnant
THANK GOD!
ANOTHER DAY, ANOTHER SCARE. IN AUGUST 2001 I WAS SURE I WAS PREGNANT. I GOT TESTED BY MY DOCTOR AND IT WAS NEGATIVE.
WOOHOO IF THERE IS ONE THING I'M NOT IT'S PREGNANT!
GOOD, BECAUSE IF I WAS, I WOULD RUN, NOT WALK, TO THE ABORTION CLINIC!
UNBEKNOWNST TO ME, I GOT PREGNANT NOT A WEEK LATER.
SOON AFTER THAT I WENT TO BURNINGMAN AND PARTIED DOWN
BINGE DRINKING
ECSTACY
DEHYDRATION
CHAIN SMOKING
CRYSTAL METH
NITROUS
MED TENT
I FEARED FOR MY LIFE AND WAS UNUSUALLY VIGILANT ABOUT EXTERNAL THREATS
ARE YOU THREATENING ME?!*
*USUALLY FINE WITH BEING THREATENED
I WAS RELIGIOUS* ABOUT USING BIRTH CONTROL. AFTER THE PILL MADE ME DEPRESSED I USED A DIAPHRAGM & SPERMICIDE.
*NO PUN INTENDED
SPERM-X
THE EFFECTIVENESS SOUNDED GOOD ENOUGH; IN RETROSPECT THEY WERE NOT!

I CAME HOME FROM BURNINGMAN AND HAD A 4-MONTH LONG BREAKDOWN. I WENT BACK TO MY DOCTOR AGAIN AND AGAIN.
I'M GOING INSAAANE!
HMM, HERE'S AN RX FOR WELLBUTRIN
AND A REFERRAL FOR A PSYCHIATRIST.
I WAS HAVING CONSTANT PANIC ATTACKS AND PRACTICALLY HALLUCINATING WITH PARANOIA. MY BOOBS KEPT HAVING STABBING PAINS.
YOU ALL HATE ME!
TATS, NO! WE ALL LOVE YOU!
I SUSPECTED I MIGHT BE PREGNANT - BUT THEN I HAD WHAT LOOKED LIKE MY PERIOD.
PHEW! IF YOU BLEED OUT YOUR VAG IT MEANS YOU'RE NOT PREGNANT!
NOT TRUE!
EVENTUALLY MY DOC TOOK BLOOD SAMPLES TO CHECK FOR THYROID, ETC. ISSUES.
EVEN THOUGH WE TESTED FOR PREGNANCY ALREADY, LET'S TEST AGAIN WHILE WE'RE AT IT.
SOON AFTER MY DOC CALLED WITH THE NEWS... I WAS VERY PREGNANT.
NONONO
IT'S NOT TRUE
I WAS ALREADY LOSING IT AND THE NOTION THERE WAS AN UNINVITED PARASITE INSIDE ME FELT RIGHT OUT OF THE MOVIE "ALIEN"
AAAA GET IT OUT!
A FRIEND CAME WITH ME TO THE ULTRASOUND. I SUSPECT THE TECHNICIAN WAS PRO-LIFE.
LOOK AT IT! HERE YOU CAN SEE IT'S TINY LITTLE HANDS AND OOH! I CAN SEE IT'S HEART BEATING!
WAAAAAAA
I SAW MY DOC TO DISCUSS MY OPTIONS. I WAS FOUR MONTHS ALONG. I SUSPECT MY DOC WAS PRO-LIFE.
OH, I'M GETTING AN ABORTION.
OR, YOU COULD KEEP IT! OR PUT IT UP FOR ADOPTION!
NO.
BUT...
SHE LEFT THE ROOM SO I COULD 'CONSIDER' - I GRABBED HER PHONE AND CALLED CLINICS UNTIL I FOUND ONE THAT WOULD TAKE ME IN MY SECOND TRIMESTER
IT COSTS HOW MUCH?!
I DON'T HAVE ANY MONEY!
IT COST THOUSANDS OF DOLLARS UP FRONT, NO COVERAGE! LUCKILY I QUALIFIED FOR ASSISTANCE.

AT FOUR MONTHS, I NEEDED A 'D&E'-DILATION AND EVACUATION. NO CLINICS IN LIBERAL SEATTLE WOULD DO IT. I FOUND ONE ON THE OUTSKIRTS OF TOWN, IN THE PROSTITUTION DISTRICT.
SHADY MOTEL
CIVILIZATION
MIDDLE OF NOWHERE
ABORTION CLINIC
THAT NIGHT, AS I WAS LOSING MY SHIT, MY BOYFRIEND AND I HAD A MATURE DISCUSSION ABOUT THE SITUATION.
THIS IS ALL YOUR FAULT!
WHAT?! THIS IS ALL YOUR FAULT!
THE NEXT FEW DAYS D R A G G E D PAST AS I WAITED FOR MY APPOINTMENTS. AT WORK MY BOSS SENT ME HOME - ONE LOOK AND HE KNEW I WASN'T WELL.
HOLE OF DESPAIR
A FRIEND DROVE ME OUT TO THE BOONIES FOR MY DILATION APPOINTMENT. I HAD A MANDATORY COUNSELING TO MAKE SURE I WAS SURE
NOW...
I'M SURE.
WELL...
I'M SURE
I WOULDN'T LIVE THROUGH 5 MORE MONTHS OF PREGNANCY AND I'M SURE I'D BRAIN-DAMAGED THE FETUS.
IT WAS THE LONGEST WAIT OF MY LIFE
Highlights
DILATION=INSERTING OSMOTIC RODS INTO MY CERVIX. THEY WOULD EXPAND OVERNIGHT TO DILATE MY CERVIX
AHHHHG
I WENT HOME AND WAITED AS THE RODS EXPANDED. FRIENDS CAME BY FOR MORAL SUPPORT. I TOOK PAINKILLERS BUT THEY BARELY MADE A DENT
AAGHKHH
THE NEXT DAY MY BOYFRIEND DROVE ME BACK OUT FOR MY EVACUATION. ANOTHER INFINITE WAIT.
Scraping & sucking
IT WAS HORRIBLE BUT THE DRUGS WERE INCREDIBLE. I FLOATED IN THE CLOUDS PAINTED ON THE CIELING
A FEW DAYS LATER I CAME HOME FROM WORK AND REALIZED I'D BEEN LACTATING
AIEEEE
INTERNALIZED MISOGENY
SEX ISSUES
MOMMY ISSUES
BODY ISSUES

IN 2001 (AGE 26) NONE OF MY FRIENDS HAD KIDS YET. I DIDN'T KNOW ANYONE WHO'D HAD AN ABORTION WHO'D TOLD ME. I DIDN'T USE THE INTERNET A TON. I THOUGHT I WAS ONE IN A MILLION
SHAME
FALLEN WOMAN
URBAN LEGENDS ABOUT GIRLS WHO DON'T KNOW THEY'RE PREGNANT
FUCKUP WHO CAN'T USE BIRTH CONTROL RIGHT!
I DIDN'T KNOW ANYONE WHO'D MISCARRIED. I DIDN'T KNOW WHAT WAS HAPPENING TO MY BODY.
LOSS
GRIEF
CONFUSION
ANXIETY
DEPRESSION
IMBALANCE
CRAZED FROM HORMONES
in your place an empty space
I SWALLOWED IT. I HAD NOWHERE TO PUT THESE EMOTIONS, AND ONE GO-TO SKILL SET FOR PAIN MANAGEMENT.
booze
pot
pills
coke
NO_2
THE LITTLE FAITH I HAD IN LIFE WAS GONE. I NEVER IMAGINED THINGS COULD FEEL SO AWFUL AND DARK.
A FEW MONTHS LATER, I DREW A COMIC ABOUT MY ABORTION.
I COULD NEVER PUBLISH THIS!
HM, WELL MAYBE ONE DAY, IF IT WAS ANONYMOUS
OR I'LL BURY IT IN A BOX AND NEVER LOOK AT IT AGAIN! (WHAT I DID, FOR 13 YEARS!)
OVER THE NEXT FEW YEARS I BECAME MORE ACTIVE ONLINE AND NOTICED A FEW WOMEN MENTION THEY'D HAD ABORTIONS. I STILL ASSUMED I WAS ONE OF THE FEW. I CHEERED FOR PRO-CHOICE BUT NEVER GOT INVOLVED
WOW SHE TALKS ABOUT BEING PRO-CHOICE RIGHT ON HER BLOG... COOL!
OK I'LL SIGN THE NARAL E-PETITION
EVERY TIME I STOPPED DRINKING, ESPECIALLY WHEN I QUIT FOR GOOD IN 2009, MY ABORTION SHAME EMERGED.
I'VE ALWAYS BEEN PRO-CHOICE
WHY DO I FEEL THIS WAY?
MURDERER
BABY KILLER
IN 2014 I DUG OUT THE COMIC I'D DRAWN OF MY ABORTION. I SHARED IT SELECTIVELY. IT BROUGHT UP SO MUCH GRIEF I WAS CRAWLING ON ALL FOURS.
DONT TALK ABOUT IT
IF I'D KEPT IT, IT WOULD BE 13 YEARS OLD! AND BRAIN DAMAGED. AND I'D BE DEAD OR LOCKED UP...
IN 2015 I DISCOVERED THE SHOUT YOUR ABORTION MOVEMENT. SO. MANY. WOMEN WERE SHARING THEIR STORIES! I LEARNED ONE IN FOUR WOMEN HAD AN ABORTION! SINCE NO ONE TALKED ABOUT IT, I HAD ASSUMED IT WAS RARE AND SHAMEFUL.
I'M... I'M... NORMAL?
PEOPLE ARE TALKING ABOUT THEIR ABORTIONS ON FACEBOOK!?
WE CAN DO THAT?
IN 2016 I WENT TO A SHOUT YOUR ABORTION RALLY. I SAW PEOPLE THERE FROM MY DAY-TO-DAY LIFE. I STOOD IN A CROWD AS WE CELEBRATED OUR CHOICES AND SOLIDARITY. I WEPT WITH RELIEF.
I DON'T HAVE TO BE ASHAMED
I FELT LIKE 1,000 TONS WERE LIFTED OFF ME AND HAVEN'T FELT THE SHAME SINCE.

I WEAR THE SHIRT I GOT AT THE S.Y.A. RALLY TO OTHER EVENTS AND MARCHES - WITH PRIDE.
EVERYONE KNOWS I HAD AN ABORTION
WOMEN HAVE RUN UP TO ME AND HUGGED ME FOR IT.
THANK YOU FOR WEARING THAT SHIRT!
I HAD ONE, TOO.
AW THANK YOU!
LIVING A RELATIVELY PRIVILEGED LIFE, THE THOUGHTS AND FEELINGS I HAD AROUND MY PREGNANCY AND ABORTION WERE THE WORST THINGS TO EVER HAPPEN TO ME.
I HAVE NEVER FELT THIS BAD
I NEVER KNEW ANYONE COULD FEEL THIS BAD
THIS AFRAID
THIS FUCKED OVER
THIS WRONG
THIS ASHAMED
THIS DARK
THIS ROTTEN
MY SOUL
I DIDN'T THINK ABORTION WAS WRONG, BUT I FELT SO BAD I REASONED I MUST BE BAD.
AS I GOT OLDER, MANY FRIENDS GOT PREGNANT AND FRIENDS LOST EMBRYOS FOR A VARIETY OF REASONS.
YOU MISCARRIED AND NOW YOU HAVE TO GET THE FETUS VACCUMED OUT? I'M SO SORRY! OH HON, THAT SOUNDS SO TRAUMATIC. ♡
HUH... MAYBE WHAT I WENT THROUGH WAS TRAUMATIC*!
*I IMAGINE CHILDBIRTH AND RAISING KIDS CAN ALSO BE TRAUMATIC!
MY FRIEND HAS BEEN SO DEPRESSED AND DEVASTATED SINCE SHE MISCARRIED. IT MAKES SENSE BIOLOGICALLY!
EVEN THOUGH I CHOSE TO HAVE AN ABORTION, MY BODY MAY HAVE STILL BEEN REALLY UPSET THAT IT 'LOST' A PREGNANCY!
I NEVER PROCESSED MY GRIEF IN A HEALTHY, CATHARTIC WAY. I BEAT MYSELF UP FOR BEING A HUMAN!
I STARTED TO SEE FIRSTHAND HOW PREGNANCY CAN AFFECT SOMEONE.
ARE YOU FUCKING WITH ME?!
BAWW
I JUST NEED A FEW MORE NAPS
OHH... OF COURSE I WAS LOSING IT!
I AM STUNNED THAT DESPITE BEING RAISED IN LIBERAL SEATTLE AND IDENTIFYING AS PRO-CHOICE, I DID NOT FIND A COMMUNITY WILLING TO ADMIT TO AND DISCUSS THEIR ABORTIONS UNTIL I WAS 40 YEARS OLD!
I'M GLAD I MADE THE CHOICE I DID!
ME TOO!
LATELY I'VE SEEN ZINES, ARTICLES, COMICS AND BOOKS WHERE PEOPLE TALK ABOUT THEIR ABORTIONS. I NOW HAVE A COLLECTION!
Shrill
Dear Doctor ♡
GREY AREA
SHOUT YOUR ABORTION NYC
I HAD AN ABORTION AND IT WAS FINE
LOUDER
MANY OF THEM SAY THAT IT WAS NOT HARD, SHAMEFUL OR REGRETTABLE - ESPECIALLY ONES THAT HAPPENED IN A POST-SECRETIVE WORLD.
HAPPY OR SAD, EASY OR HARD, EARLY OR LATE TERM, HAVING AN ABORTION IS OKAY.
IT IS YOUR ABORTION. YOU GET TO TALK ABOUT IT. THIS SHOUT YOUR ABORTION SLOGAN SUMS IT UP:
OUR STORIES ARE OURS TO TELL.
THIS IS MINE.

LGBTQ+ RIGHTS
CLIMATE CHANGE IS REAL
FIGHT HATE
NOT MY PRESIDENT
BLACK LIVES MATTER
PUSSY GRABS BACK
EQUAL RIGHTS NOW
EVERYBODY KNOWS I HAD AN ABORTION
TATS

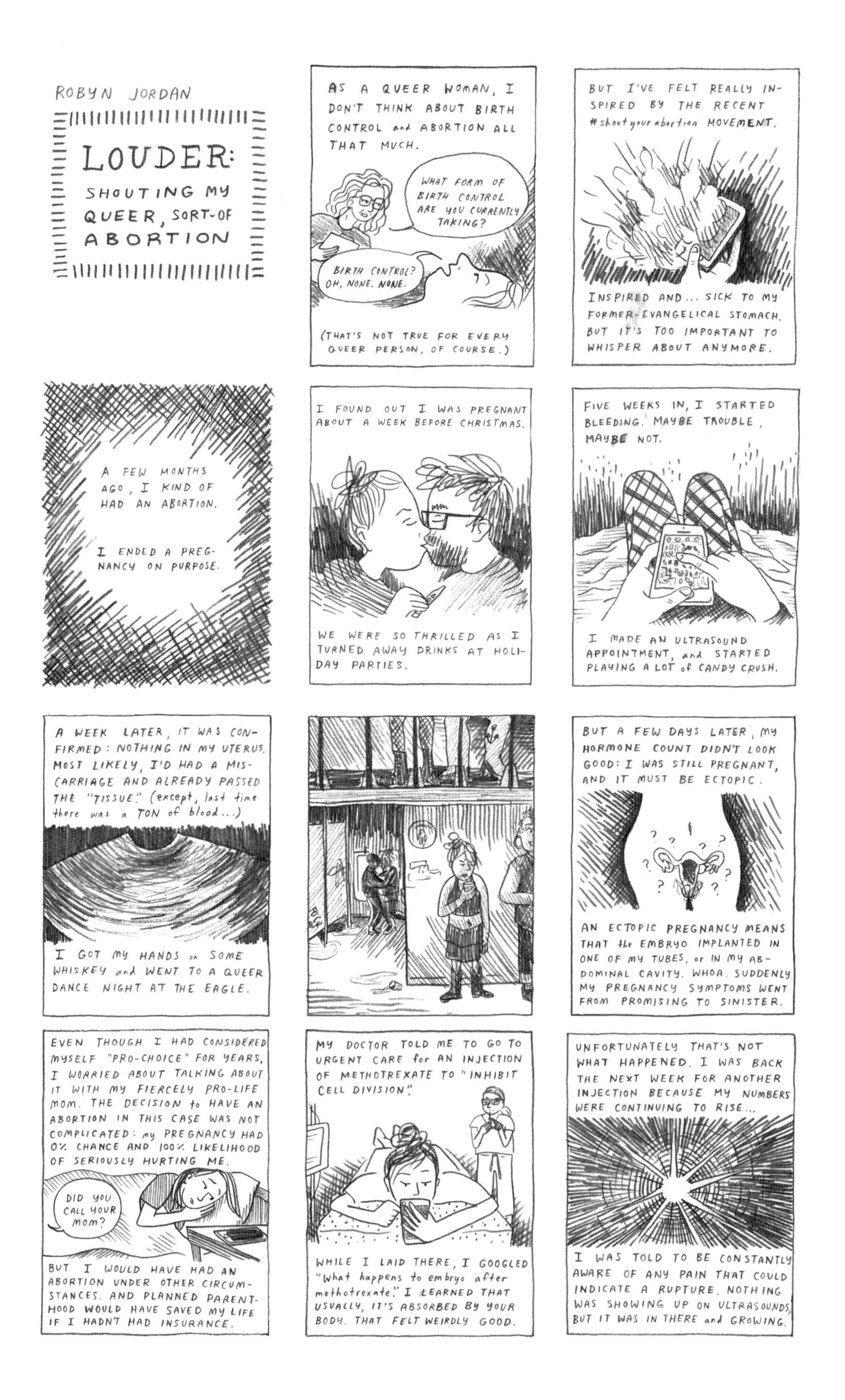
ROBYN JORDAN
LOUDER: SHOUTING MY QUEER, SORT-OF ABORTION
AS A QUEER WOMAN, I DON'T THINK ABOUT BIRTH CONTROL and ABORTION ALL THAT MUCH.
WHAT FORM OF BIRTH CONTROL ARE YOU CURRENTLY TAKING?
BIRTH CONTROL? OH, NONE. NONE.
(THAT'S NOT TRUE FOR EVERY QUEER PERSON, OF COURSE.)
BUT I'VE FELT REALLY INSPIRED BY THE RECENT #shoutyourabortion MOVEMENT.
INSPIRED AND... SICK TO MY FORMER-EVANGELICAL STOMACH. BUT IT'S TOO IMPORTANT TO WHISPER ABOUT ANYMORE.
A FEW MONTHS AGO, I KIND OF HAD AN ABORTION.
I ENDED A PREGNANCY ON PURPOSE.
I FOUND OUT I WAS PREGNANT ABOUT A WEEK BEFORE CHRISTMAS.
WE WERE SO THRILLED AS I TURNED AWAY DRINKS AT HOLIDAY PARTIES.
FIVE WEEKS IN, I STARTED BLEEDING. MAYBE TROUBLE, MAYBE NOT.
I MADE AN ULTRASOUND APPOINTMENT, and STARTED PLAYING A LOT of CANDY CRUSH.
A WEEK LATER, IT WAS CONFIRMED: NOTHING IN MY UTERUS. MOST LIKELY, I'D HAD A MISCARRIAGE AND ALREADY PASSED THE "TISSUE." (except, last time there was a TON of blood...)
I GOT MY HANDS on SOME WHISKEY and WENT TO A QUEER DANCE NIGHT AT THE EAGLE.
BUT A FEW DAYS LATER, MY HORMONE COUNT DIDN'T LOOK GOOD: I WAS STILL PREGNANT, AND IT MUST BE ECTOPIC.
AN ECTOPIC PREGNANCY MEANS THAT the EMBRYO IMPLANTED IN ONE OF MY TUBES, or IN MY ABDOMINAL CAVITY. WHOA. SUDDENLY MY PREGNANCY SYMPTOMS WENT FROM PROMISING TO SINISTER.
EVEN THOUGH I HAD CONSIDERED MYSELF "PRO-CHOICE" FOR YEARS, I WORRIED ABOUT TALKING ABOUT IT WITH MY FIERCELY PRO-LIFE MOM. THE DECISION to HAVE AN ABORTION IN THIS CASE WAS NOT COMPLICATED: my PREGNANCY HAD 0% CHANCE AND 100% LIKELIHOOD OF SERIOUSLY HURTING ME.
DID YOU CALL YOUR MOM?
BUT I WOULD HAVE HAD AN ABORTION UNDER OTHER CIRCUMSTANCES. AND PLANNED PARENTHOOD WOULD HAVE SAVED MY LIFE IF I HADN'T HAD INSURANCE.
MY DOCTOR TOLD ME TO GO TO URGENT CARE for AN INJECTION OF METHOTREXATE TO "INHIBIT CELL DIVISION."
WHILE I LAID THERE, I GOOGLED "what happens to embryo after methotrexate." I LEARNED THAT USUALLY, IT'S ABSORBED BY YOUR BODY. THAT FELT WEIRDLY GOOD.
UNFORTUNATELY THAT'S NOT WHAT HAPPENED. I WAS BACK THE NEXT WEEK FOR ANOTHER INJECTION BECAUSE MY NUMBERS WERE CONTINUING TO RISE...
I WAS TOLD TO BE CONSTANTLY AWARE OF ANY PAIN THAT COULD INDICATE A RUPTURE. NOTHING WAS SHOWING UP ON ULTRASOUNDS, BUT IT WAS IN THERE and GROWING.

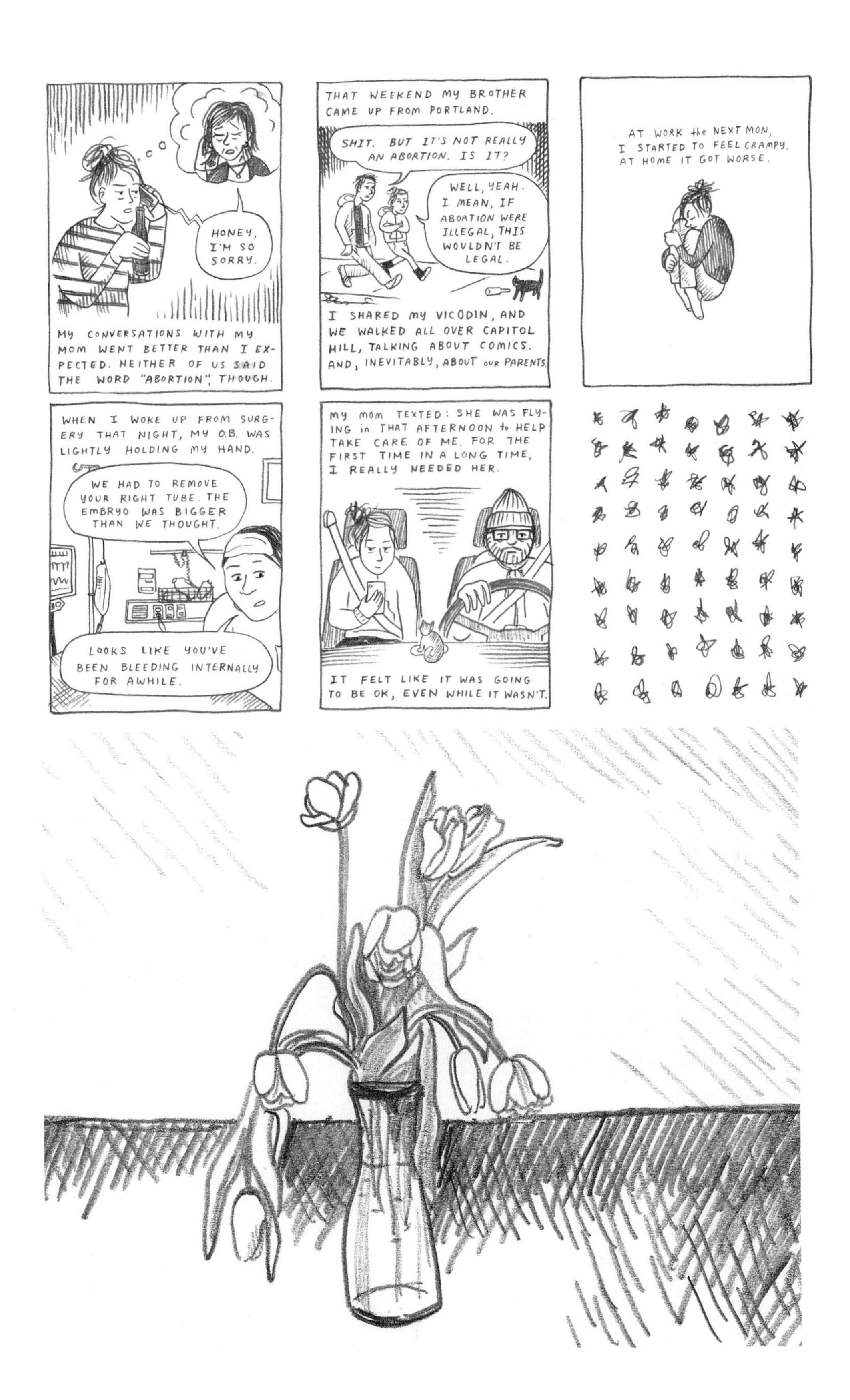
HONEY, I'M SO SORRY.
MY CONVERSATIONS WITH MY MOM WENT BETTER THAN I EXPECTED. NEITHER OF US SAID THE WORD "ABORTION", THOUGH.
THAT WEEKEND MY BROTHER CAME UP FROM PORTLAND.
SHIT. BUT IT'S NOT REALLY AN ABORTION. IS IT?
WELL, YEAH. I MEAN, IF ABORTION WERE ILLEGAL, THIS WOULDN'T BE LEGAL.
I SHARED MY VICODIN, AND WE WALKED ALL OVER CAPITOL HILL, TALKING ABOUT COMICS. AND, INEVITABLY, ABOUT OUR PARENTS.
AT WORK THE NEXT MON, I STARTED TO FEEL CRAMPY. AT HOME IT GOT WORSE.
WHEN I WOKE UP FROM SURGERY THAT NIGHT, MY O.B. WAS LIGHTLY HOLDING MY HAND.
WE HAD TO REMOVE YOUR RIGHT TUBE. THE EMBRYO WAS BIGGER THAN WE THOUGHT.
LOOKS LIKE YOU'VE BEEN BLEEDING INTERNALLY FOR AWHILE.
MY MOM TEXTED: SHE WAS FLYING IN THAT AFTERNOON TO HELP TAKE CARE OF ME. FOR THE FIRST TIME IN A LONG TIME, I REALLY NEEDED HER.
IT FELT LIKE IT WAS GOING TO BE OK, EVEN WHILE IT WASN'T.

ABORTION IS NORMAL
ABORTION IS NORMAL
ABORTION IS NORMAL
ABORTION IS NORMAL
ABORTION IS NORMAL
ABORTION IS NORMAL
ABORTION IS NORMAL
ABORTION IS NORMAL
ABORTION IS NORMAL
ABORTION IS NORMAL
ABORTION IS NORMAL
ABORTION IS NORMAL
ABORTION IS NORMAL
ABORTION IS NORMAL

ABORTION IS NORMAL
ABORTION IS NORMAL
ABORTION IS NORMAL
ABORTION IS NORMAL
E Pine St
Pine St
ABORTION IS NORMAL
ABORTION IS NORMAL
ABORTION IS NORMAL
STAFF ONLY
ABORTION IS NORMAL
ABORTION IS NORMAL
ABORTION IS NORMAL
ABORTION IS NORMAL
ABORTION IS NORMAL
ABORTION IS NORMAL

PROVIDERS

without them we'd have nothing to shout

MY MOTHER HAD A SAFE BUT ILLEGAL ABORTION WHEN SHE WAS 18 & A FRESHMAN IN COLLEGE.

SHE WENT ON TO FINISH SCHOOL, HAVE A PLANNED FAMILY, & FULFILL HER LIFELONG DREAM OF BECOMING A DOCTOR.

me & Mom, 1975

MY DEEPEST GRATITUDE TO THE DOCTOR WHO HELPED MY MOM EARLY ONE MORNING IN 1961,

FOR PUTTING YOUR PRACTICE ON THE LINE...

FOR GETTING MY BRILLIANT MOTHER'S LIFE BACK ON TRACK...

AND FOR MY EXISTENCE.

Ellen Forney

THEY WILL PROVIDE

Abortion providers take care of us when nobody else will, and they're fighting for their right to continue doing so—no matter what.

It's hard to imagine what would motivate someone to work in abortion care when it seems like any other job in health care would be easier. The legislative environment surrounding abortion is erratic and hostile, most people who walk through the clinic doors are under incredible stress, and every interaction a provider has with a patient is intrinsically high-stakes. While all other sorts of doctors are lauded as lifesavers, abortion care providers have been so demonized by a small segment of the population that managing harassment and the constant threat of violence is a part of the job. On top of all this, there's the actual work, and one could reasonably assume that performing abortions all day is somewhat grim.

In the few years since SYA began, people who work at abortion clinics all over the country have become my friends and colleagues. Although in some ways their jobs are unfathomably difficult, I have never met anyone as joyfully, unequivocally committed to their work as abortion care providers. Working in abortion care means encountering patients in the most potent, critical, messy moments of their lives. In some cases, providers bear witness to incalculable loss; in others, they liberate their patients from a future that might have crushed them. In every single case, their role in a patient's life is transformational. The providers I know don't provide abortion *in spite of* the existential weight of their work; they have chosen to provide abortion because they know that abortion is everything.

The voices of people who have actually had abortions have long been suppressed by those looking to keep real, human perspectives out of the abortion debate. Abortion providers have been silenced as well, which is ultimately just another way to keep the truth out of this conversation and keep our stories untold. Abortion providers are expert witnesses. They've seen the way abortion actually works in countless people's lives and have had their convictions on the subject tested in ways that others simply can't imagine. As light floods into this conversation, more and more providers are speaking out. They've got a lot to say, because they have seen it all.

Although abortion care in the U.S. is nearly synonymous with Planned Parenthood, 60 percent of the abortions in the U.S. are performed by independent abortion care providers. Independent clinics (or "indies") are smaller and more institutionally nimble than Planned Parenthood, which allows them to focus on meeting the specific needs of their communities and providing a wider range of care, such as second trimester abortion and LGBT health services. The flipside is that indies are much more vulnerable to attack from anti-choice legislation—like TRAP (Targeted Regulation of Abortion Provider) laws, which make it difficult or impossible for clinics to provide abortion services—and they're typically more under-resourced than larger clinics. In this section, we chose to highlight four independent care providers, all of whom work in the Deep South—because they're providing care that nobody else will, and most people don't even know they exist.

To learn more about locating and supporting independent abortion care providers, see the Abortion Care Network in the Resources section, page 232.

Essay and interviews by Amelia Bonow.

DR. WILLIE PARKER

Born and raised in Alabama, Dr. Willie Parker made his way out of southern poverty and through medical school, eventually landing his dream job as an OB-GYN with a faculty appointment at the University of Hawaii. A man of deep faith, Dr. Parker avoided performing abortions, feeling he lacked moral certainty on the issue. In 2002, Dr. Parker had a realization: people who weren't able to have abortions were suffering, and he had the power to help them. Dr. Parker returned to the South and became a full-time abortion care provider, serving the most disenfranchised people in the country. Today, Dr. Parker is one of the most vocal, visible providers in his field, guided by an absolute conviction that he is doing the Lord's work.

Amelia: You've said that it was relatively easy to avoid practicing abortion while you were an OB-GYN, which speaks to the fact that it's treated as a fundamentally separate discipline. What are your thoughts about that separation? And do you think folks shouldn't be OB-GYNs if they don't want to practice abortion, since people needing abortions is a big part of the deal?

Dr. Parker: As far as where abortion is situated within reproductive health care and who is trained to do it: there is what's ideal, and there's what is. Ideally, I think there should be no equivocation on what constitutes reproductive health care, and that reproductive health care includes abortion. In the medical community, we say that women have a right to health care. As physicians and as healers, we take an oath to do no harm, and to practice beneficence—to do good. I think to deny a woman an abortion when she needs one constitutes harm, and to provide abortions for a woman when she needs one is beneficence. It's to do good.

Something that one in four women in this country needs by the time they're age 45 is essential health care. And I think that people choosing to be OB-GYNs need to understand what the discipline includes. Not to be crass, but someone who has serious issues with feces can't be a gastroenterologist. I'm not at all equivocating between products of conception and—

Amelia: You're just saying that it's part of the deal.

Dr. Parker: Yes. It's part of what you do. And people always ask me, "How do you do what you do?" Well, I do it very well for women, and I do it with a great deal of satisfaction. A lot of what people are distracted by is the stigmatized aspect of dealing with human tissue and fetal tissue. That's not the core of what I do. I do remove pregnancies, but ultimately my job is to help women by providing them care that they need, that other people do not make available to them, and I am very satisfied by that.

Amelia: I appreciated the part in Dawn Porter's documentary *Trapped* where you've just performed an abortion and you're sifting through the products of pregnancy in the sink, and it's obvious that the person shooting it is not expecting you to let them tape that, and you're like, "No, I want you to see this." Can you talk a little bit about why that is?

Dr. Parker: I'm under the impression that the truth will do, and I think that we are in this position right now with abortion stigma and abortion bans because we have not trusted people to deal with the complexity and the reality of life. Pregnancies often end, either involuntary by miscarriage or intentionally because a person didn't desire to be pregnant in the first place, or they did but they're too ill to continue. At the end of the day, I think our inability or our lack of willingness to deal with the reality of what abortion is, or at least pregnancy interruption, has left a huge vacuum that's been filled with misconceptions, lies, stigmatizing, and shame. The antidote to a lie is always the truth, and the truth will do. I figure that if we say, "trust women," we might as well say, let's trust everybody to see this for what it is and then deal with the reality.

Amelia: Another truth that's missing from the conversation is that so many of us have had them! I think anti-choice people honestly believe that they don't know anybody who has had an abortion, which is just not true. They're only able to keep believing that because the women in their lives who have had abortions haven't been able to trust them with that truth. But it feels like that's starting to shift. You've now been performing abortions for 15 years. How have you seen the landscape change culturally in that time?

Dr. Parker: On one hand, I've seen more people who can get pregnant telling their stories. I've seen more providers starting to be public in their identity. At the same time, I've seen people who are opposed to abortion double down. We're at the precipice of abortion potentially being outlawed by the reversal of *Roe*, and we've seen an evisceration of the provisions of *Roe* at the state level, because political ideologues have sought to vet themselves politically as conservatives by stigmatizing and shaming reproductive health care in the form of abortion. So, we're in this funky place, because it's incontrovertible how common abortion is, and more folks are finding their voices through work like yours and mine—people who have had abortions and providers like me. And yet we've never been closer to abortion being made illegal. It's very Dickensian. It's the best of times, it's the worst of times.

Amelia: Your book, *Life's Work: A Moral Argument for Choice*, came out in spring 2017. What is your greatest hope for what that book has done and will continue to do and what are you working on next?

Dr. Parker: On April 4, the book will have been out a year. That date has salience for me not only as the launch of my first book, but also as the anniversary of Dr. King's assassination. I see my empowerment as an individual who stands in this space as a health care professional, without any limitations on my trajectory, as the fulfillment of Dr. King's legacy. The book has done well and has been a tool for fostering the conversation, and my hope is that the book speaks from both sides of the divide in a way that is rooted in integrity.

The next book is called *Man's Work: Rescuing Masculinity from Patriarchy* and it revolves around my belief that patriarchy is the original hierarchical relationship, and that because that relationship is constructed, it can be deconstructed, and that's our work.

Amelia: What does a healthy version of masculinity look like to you?

Dr. Parker: A healthy version of masculinity is one that does not define itself by the subordination of someone or something else. I think that that is learned behavior. The socialization around being a boy or a girl or a man or a woman starts when the health care provider looks between the baby's legs and says, "it's a boy" or "it's a girl." Automatically the cultural expectations begin to get established, and we give little boys toy guns and we give little girls dolls, and never the twain shall meet. I'm saying that a human rights framework would say, "How do we raise healthy human beings?"

A positive masculinity or manhood would be an expression of masculinity that is informed by human rights, meaning rights that are not conferred by or derived from the state, as Dr. King would say, but they're rights that should be guaranteed by the state, and that the guarantee of those rights should not be distributed by the accident of birth, whether you're male or female, or whether you understand yourself as something totally different from the two.

Frederick Douglass said that it's easier to raise healthy boys than to fix broken men, and I think our pathways to masculinity—

Amelia: Damn! He was on that.

Dr. Parker: He was on that. He is one of my original feminist heroes. Frederick Douglass had the presence of mind to realize that the same forces that oppressed him on the basis of his color were the same ones that oppressed women. He was a champion of suffrage. His lived experience was that of a black man; he understood that slavery was a violation of human rights, and that disenfranchisement of women was also a violation of human rights. Like Dr. King says, he had dual concerns because he refused to segregate his human rights concerns.

Amelia: I know you drive around a lot and I want to know what you like to listen to in the car, because I've seen you on the dance floor.

Dr. Parker: I love music. A long time ago I decided to dance like nobody is looking. It may be that's what it looks like when I'm dancing. I'm dancing like nobody is looking.

Amelia: They make that poster after you?

Dr. Parker: Maybe so.

Amelia: You're an inspiration.

Dr. Parker: I listen to music, but for me, the drive between clinics is a contemplative and meditative space where I nourish my intellect and my soul, so I listen to a lot of books on tape. I just listened to *The New Jim Crow* and *Slavery by Another Name*. I have lots of recordings of Dr. King and Malcolm X. I look to them because although we are in unique circumstances, they're nothing new, and we need to invoke the wisdom of people who had to be in it for the long haul. I listen to the thoughts of people who envisioned things beyond the world that they were living in. In some ways, we live now in a world that Dr. King hoped for, but in other ways, it's beyond what he could have imagined. They didn't know nothing about the internet, right?

Amelia: Right.

Dr. Parker: So it's sort of a trick question... like, "What do you think Dr. King's email address was?" I don't know, probably something, something, mlk@sclc.org. Anyway, all to say you have to be present and your time is your time. This is the moment that we are all living in together. And I want to leave the world better than I found it.

Amelia: What inspires you to continue your work?

Dr. Parker: There's a Jewish wisdom from the Talmud. It says, "We're not obligated to finish the work, but neither are we free to abandon it." Even though in my lifetime, which I hope is a long life, I might not see the actual full-scale empowerment and liberation of women and people who need abortions, I'm not free to abandon the work.

I'm inspired by the present moment. I'm well aware that natural longevity means at 55 years old, it's almost a certainty that I have more years behind me than I have in front of me. I measure my life by the number of times I get to see the leaves change. Fall is my favorite season. How many more times do I get to see the leaves change? A friend sent me a birthday card that said, "Congratulations on completing another 365 day trip around the sun." If you think about that, the earth isn't moving up or down. It's just going around the sun. It's not getting older or younger. It's just fulfilling its mission. If I look at my life not as getting young or older, but just as a matter of, how am I spending my time on the trip around the sun? That's important. I'm enjoying the journey. There's no time like the present to do the things that you find meaningful. ■

MARVA N. SADLER

Whole Woman's Health is a feminist healthcare organization that provides comprehensive gynecological care, including abortion, at eight sites all over the country. Marva N. Sadler oversees WWH's four Texas clinics—located in Fort Worth, McAllen, Austin, and San Antonio—as well as the WWH clinic in Baltimore.

Amelia: Overseeing five clinics sounds like a lot. What does your job entail?

Marva: I work with the clinic managers to ensure that they have everything they need for day-to-day operations. I also work quite closely with most of the operational elements within the clinic as far as managing and tracking our patient volume to include tracking revenue and expenses for the clinic. Beyond all the regular operational things, I step in when unexpected things happen. I'm constantly figuring out how to make all of our clinics comply with TRAP laws so that we can continue providing safe, quality abortion care to our communities. A related part of my job is doctor scheduling, making sure we have a provider available at each site. In another field that would be a simple administrative job, but because of TRAP laws such as the admitting privileges law, we find it difficult sometimes to schedule physicians.

Amelia: Can you explain the admitting privileges law in terms of what it pretends to do versus the actual effect?

Marva: Well thankfully, because we won the *Woman's Health v. Texas* Supreme Court case in 2016, the admitting privileges requirement is gone. Proponents of the law said it would increase the safety of procedures because the doctors would have admitting privileges to the hospital closest to the clinic if there was an emergency. One thing that you have to understand is that less than 1 percent of our patients are seen for complications or need care outside of the clinic.

Ultimately, an emergency situation is handled the same way whether a doctor has admitting privileges or not, because the doctor that's seeing the patient in the clinic is not going to be the doctor that goes to the hospital to actually see the patient there.

The real intent of the law was to make doctors unable to legally perform abortion care.

Amelia: Did you see providers choosing to stop working in abortion care because TRAP laws made it so difficult to practice?

Marva: I saw many doctors be forced out of abortion care because of TRAP laws. There were doctors who absolutely wanted to provide services for women but were unable to obtain privileges to hospitals because they did abortions. It was a loophole inside a catch-22. Hospitals would refuse to even accept their applications in some instances.

Amelia: How long have you been working in abortion care and what were you doing before?

Marva: I've been in abortion care for almost 13 years and with Whole Woman's Health for almost 10 years now. Before that, I started as a paramedic, working on the truck, then eventually made my way into many other places, including the emergency room.

I worked at a women's prison for a little while, and then stumbled into a job at Planned Parenthood in Waco. It was not intentional. I just took a job and as soon as I got started, I realized what the fight actually was about, and I just got swept in.

Amelia: What swept you in?

Marva: I honestly think it was the protestors. Before my job at Planned Parenthood, I just had no idea how bad it was, that it was a full-time job for some folks to interfere with a woman's choice. I was raised in a house full of women. I thought that you got pregnant, you decided what you wanted to do, you got up, you did it, and that was the end of the discussion. When I saw how bad the situation was with the protesters, I realized that I had the ability to really help, and I knew I couldn't walk away.

I'd heard a lot about Whole Woman's Health and about Amy [Hagstrom Miller] and was very drawn to the care model and ensuring that women were treated with compassion and respect. It's all about meeting women where they are and going the extra mile for each and every patient if that's what's needed, being able to make adjustments and turn on a dime in order to give everybody what they need.

Of course, we have policies and procedures and guidelines, but at the end of the day when something falls out of those parameters, I know that I am never turning a patient away, and that me and my team are going to figure it out for her together. And my coworkers are my family. I just know that I can call on them when I need something for my patient, and we're going to make it happen together. We all show up to support each other and we know that we are going to change lives together every single day.

Amelia: How much have you seen the culture of abortion care change, both in terms of people being more open about their abortions and in terms of providers being more open and positive in the way they talk about the work?

Marva: Twelve years ago when I started, it was a really big deal to say the word "abortion." You didn't say it, or you could only say it in certain situations. The movement has changed a lot, and providers are much more openly abortion positive now. I've also seen a great change in the age of our providers. A lot of young folks who are coming out of school want to do abortion work and are asking to do abortion work and making their own training plans and training themselves. I've seen the average age in Texas of our providers range from 60-70 to 30 and 40. Which is great because it feels like at some point, I can retire and not do this anymore, because there are other folks coming along that can take it forward.

But we've gotta keep pushing. We can't let the conversation die, we can't let the anti's control the conversation. What you guys are doing right now is so super important—we've just gotta keep talking about it. ■

DR. YASHICA ROBINSON

Dr. Yashica Robinson is an OB-GYN with a private practice in Huntsville, Alabama, as well as an abortion care provider at the Alabama Women's Center.

Amelia: Between providing abortion and your work as an OB-GYN, you see people through all sorts of different situations. Did you start out as an OB-GYN and then get into abortion care, or vice versa?

Dr. Robinson: I initially decided that I wanted to be an obstetrician-gynecologist, and I wanted to work primarily with teenagers. I was a teen mom myself, and I felt like the medical professionals that I interacted with at that time really had the power to make me or break me. The people around me at that time could have either lifted me up and told me that I could have a child and still achieve my dreams, or they could have been like all the naysayers and told me that continuing my pregnancy would basically mean that my life was over. I wanted to be in the position to lift somebody up who is in a similar situation, so I went into obstetrics and gynecology and, incidentally, abortion care is part of that. And I respect that. Women have the right to choose what they would like to do, I'm just there to help them make that decision and get through it safely.

I've come to realize that in just listening to patients, respecting their decisions, and helping them to get through that choice without judging them...you can really empower someone deeply in a life-changing way.

Amelia: You're seeing all sorts of people, from people who might have come a very long way to have an abortion to someone who is joyfully celebrating a birth. You must see and experience a huge range of emotions day to day.

Dr. Robinson: Yes, it is a range, but also it all feels connected. I guess the best way to describe it is that I feel like I'm helping women celebrate life in either capacity, either in the abortion clinic or when somebody is having a baby.

Often when somebody has an abortion, it's the same celebration, it's the same joy, it's the same relief that is present when I'm helping a woman have a baby. Being able to be there for women, allowing them to exercise their right to choose, and then seeing their relief and their gratitude when they leave the clinic...it's overwhelming.

Amelia: Abortion is a radical act of self-care for a lot of people. And I think for a lot of people, especially young people, choosing to have an abortion is the first time that they've ever been allowed to make a choice that's completely self-determined. How incredible that no matter what somebody chooses to do, you get to say to them, "You can do this, and I'm going to help you."

Dr. Robinson: One of the things that I think that I enjoy the most—a good example of this was a young lady that I took care of just yesterday. She came through the clinic, and she's talking to me and I can see that she feels like she's already been judged so much. Maybe she's even judging herself more harshly than the people around her are judging her. However, just being with her, releasing her from that, and letting her know, "This is your decision, you don't owe anybody any explanation, and what you choose is absolutely okay." And just in that moment, she decided she could just be quiet, have her procedure done, and leave with dignity. ■

DALTON JOHNSON

Dalton Johnson is the administrator and owner of the Alabama Women's Center in Huntsville, Alabama, which is north Alabama's only abortion provider.

Amelia: In the last few years, TRAP laws have forced the closure of dozens of abortion clinics in southern states. For those of you who have managed to stay open, TRAP laws still make it incredibly difficult for you to provide services. Can you explain some of the ways TRAP laws have impacted your work in Alabama?

Dalton: The goal of a TRAP law is not to make women safer; it is to close abortion clinics and to make it difficult or impossible for women to access abortion.

Right now, we're the only provider in the state that goes to the legal limit, which is 21 weeks and six days, so we have women coming to us from Louisiana, Mississippi, and Tennessee. We have women coming from eight, 10 hours away seeking our services. They have to find the money for the abortion, as well as childcare, transportation, and lodging. In the state of Alabama, the 48-hour waiting period is really, really heartbreaking because even though we have a local provider that's available pretty much every day of the week, patients have to wait 48-hours in between their two appointments. Plenty of women can't afford two days in a hotel, and they normally have to go and come back. And a lot of times, they just don't make it back within the time period.

We had one patient last Thursday who didn't make it back in time. When she made it to us, she was two days too far along for us to provide her abortion. It really, really hurts to see that because even if you try to scramble and help her figure out somewhere to go, there's just no place in this geographical area that you can send her. They're looking at traveling halfway across the country in order to get the services that they need, just because she's two days past the cutoff. We're asking people to climb a mountain in order to access these services, especially when you're talking about the second trimester.

It's definitely been a struggle. In 2001 we got licensed in our old location. But then, due to TRAP laws, we were forced to move, buy a whole new facility, retrofit that out, and then reopen. That facility was licensed in 2014. Then last year, the state legislature passed a law saying that the clinic couldn't be within 2,000 feet of a school, treating us like sex offenders. We were able to get a temporary stay on that in federal court.

It's just kind of one thing after another, but we're battling through. We're gonna do whatever it takes to stay open and provide abortions.

Amelia: How did you come to this work? At what point did you decide that you wanted to help women in this incredibly vulnerable time of their lives, in this unbelievably volatile political context, and accept the risks and sacrifices that you do in order to provide abortion in the Deep South?

Dalton: I was bitten by the bug. Coming out of grad school with an MBA, I was approached by a physician who had always provided abortions in his private practice and who wanted to get a clinic license. I did the legwork to help him get licensed, he put up the money, and we became partners. Unfortunately, a couple years later, Dr. Palmer passed. At that point the work had become incredibly meaningful to me, and I just decided to carry the torch, and I've been doing it ever since. It's a passion.

Luckily, I now have a great business partner in Dr. Robinson. She is the only [abortion-care providing] physician in the entire state of Alabama with hospital admitting privileges She also runs a full-service OB-GYN clinic on the other side of town. Of course, we'd love to have all of it happening underneath one roof, but due to the hostile environment, we're not able to do that, even though they still protest or picket her private office five days a week.

Amelia: Her OB-GYN office?

Dalton: Yeah, the clinic where abortion services are not even being performed. Just because they know that she supports the right to choose and helps women in whatever that choice may be.

Amelia: Wow.

Dalton: These anti-choice people, they don't care about women's circumstances, about what situations they're in. They don't even let a woman continue her pregnancy in peace if the provider of their choosing happens to be pro-choice.

Amelia: The things y'all are up against day to day are just unimaginable. What keeps you going?

Dalton: I mean, one reason I keep going is because I don't know who would take care of these folks if we didn't. And what is the point of abortion being technically legal if there is no place or people to provide the service?

But really, I keep going because it just does something to me, knowing that I'm standing up for my daughter, for my mother, for my sister. You gotta stand up. You gotta really stand up and fight for what you believe in, especially now. That's what we're doing at the Alabama Women's Center. ■

SYA SUGGESTS: Life's Work: A Moral Argument for Choice *by Dr. Willie Parker is an excellent tool for starting honest, respectful conversations about abortion. For more from Marva, Dalton, and Dr. Parker, check out* Trapped, *Dawn Porter's 2016 documentary about how TRAP laws have affected providers in the Deep South. Organize a screening with friends or on your campus to help get the conversation started!*

You don’t need to have had an abortion of your own to help normalize the conversation.

All the materials you see in this section are available for free on our website.

And remember: whether you’re postering your campus or projecting onto the side of a building, guerrilla tactics require planning. Stay alert, trust your gut, know your rights, and don’t do anything that makes you feel unsafe.

Recto hilo
INSPIRATION
we have ideas

BUTTONS

Buttons start conversations. It's easy to pop them on if we feel like talking, or take them off if we don't.

IN LOVING MEMORY
ATTITUDE
IS
EVERYTHING
GEORGE R. TILLER, M.D.
SEATTLE
WASHINGTON
FUCK THE PATRIARCHY
CJB
i ♥ my local abortion provider
abortion
#SHOUT YOUR ABORTION
ABORTION IS FREEDOM
FUCK THE PATRIARCHY
HAVE A DAY.
SHOUT YOUR ABORTION

ART BY **TATIANA GILL**

ART BY **ANDREW LAMB**

POSTERS

SYA posters have popped up in galleries, abortion clinics, and on telephone poles all over the country.

RECOVERY ROOM AT **CHOICES, MEMPHIS CENTER FOR REPRODUCTIVE HEALTH.**

OUR
STORIES
ARE OURS
TO TELL
#SHOUTYOURABORTION
EVERYONE
KNOWS
I HAD AN
ABORTION

ABORTION
IS NORMAL
EVERYONE
KNOWS
I HAD AN
ABORTION

SHOUT YOUR
ABORTION
#SHOUTYOURABORTION
La vie en rose
Je voudrais un pain au chocolat

WOMEN'S MARCH SEATTLE, 2017.

ABORTION IS NORMAL ABORTION
IS NORMAL ABORTION IS NORMAL
OUR
STORIES
ARE OURS
TO TELL
Bäst

THIS IS NOT
A DEBATE
SHOUT YOUR ABORTION SHOUT
YOUR ABORTION SHOUT YOUR
EVERYONE
KNOWS
I HAD AN
BORTION

WHEAT-PASTED MURALS BY **NO TOUCHING GROUND**

BENSON
GROCERY
OCT 16-31
CAN CAN presents
THIS IS HALLOWEEN
@ THE TRIPLE DOOR
EVERYONE KNOWS I HAD AN ABORTION
IF YOU NEED
IF YOU NEED A PLACE TO STAY
SLEEP
espresso
Vivace
una bella tazza di caffe
espresso roasting &
preparation specialists
CHASE
EVERYONE
KNOWS
I HAD AN
ABORTION

PROJE

Projections take up a lot of space in a dramatic way without touching anything.

CTIONS
KNOWS
HAD AN
BORTION

On June 27, 2016, the Supreme Court announced its ruling in *Whole Woman's Health v. Hellerstedt*, striking down a set of restrictions that had decimated abortion access across southern states. That evening, SYA mounted projections in New York, Chicago, Los Angeles, San Antonio, Seattle, and Portland. The reel was projected onto the exteriors of landmarks, abandoned buildings, art galleries, music venues, and, after one woman was unable to secure a venue, a home in suburban San Antonio.

EVERYON
KNOWS

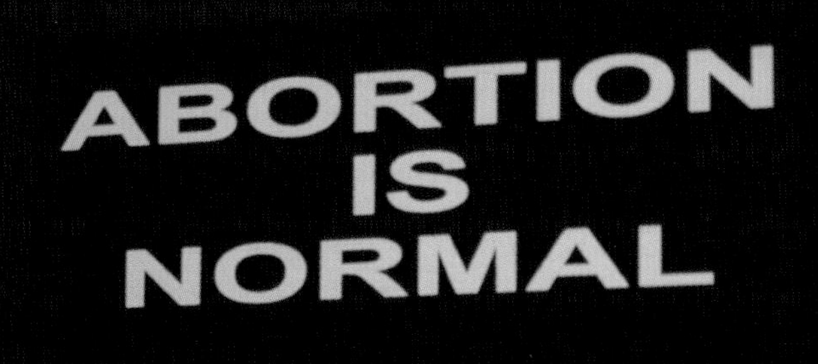
ABORTION
IS
NORMAL

EVERYONE KNOWS I HAD AN ABORTION
ABORTION IS NORMAL.
THIS IS NOT A DEBATE.
OUR STORIES ARE OURS TO TELL.
Everit St
ONE WAY

EVERYONE
KNOWS
I HAD AN
306

EVERYONE
KNOWS

KNOWS
I HAD AN
ABORTION

EVERYONE
KNOWS
I HAD AN
ABORTION
306

GLAMORIZING ABORTION

If you grew up sometime in the last few decades in a pro-choice household, you likely learned that abortion is between a woman and her doctor. That phrase is a literal articulation of our right to privacy and an indignant rejection of government intervention in our reproductive decisions. But at some point, the fact that our abortions are nobody else's business got muddied up with the notion that we should keep our abortions a secret, and the anti-choice movement began leveraging our desperation for privacy against us. Simultaneously, they rebranded abortion as murder and began systematically terrorizing people who disagreed. They made the word itself untouchable, because they knew it would be impossible to advocate for something that we couldn't even say.

This is why many of us grew up talking about choice without talking about abortion. This is why so many of us have learned to advocate for reproductive rights without discussing our own reproductive experiences. This is why so many of us are desensitized to gruesome anti-choice propaganda but find positive messages about abortion to be somewhat shocking.

Even among proudly pro-choice folks who live in political message tees, wearing a garment that says the word "abortion" is a bold move. Wearing a T-shirt that announces to the world that you've had an abortion is nothing short of radical. And wearing a popsicle-colored silk muumuu with floral epaulettes and lettering that reads "abortion is normal"? Wait, what?

Abortion couture might strike you as too edgy, too frivolous, too absurd; it might seem pointless or, worse, potentially damaging. We've all internalized the idea that if we speak about our abortions without contrition, seriousness, and self-flagellation, our stories will become anti-choice ammunition. We've been told that the worst thing we could ever do is glamorize abortion.

Here's the thing: the anti-choice movement has baited us into playing a game of respectability politics, and the game is rigged. They will never respect us, no matter how small we make ourselves and how sorry we pretend to be. So we might as well just talk about our abortions however we want, and the truth is, a lot of us are jubilant. A lot of us are proud of the people our abortions have allowed us to become. That's not just okay, it's revolutionary.

Legislative progress is the actualization of change that has already taken shape in many forms of culture; artists and activists are light years ahead of lawmakers. We want to see abortion everywhere: in galleries, on television, tattooed on our bodies, written in the sky. Making art is serious work. And if our tactics are so constrained by a triage mindset that we stop making things, we'll have relinquished our greatest power: our ability to shine. Loving ourselves defiantly, in spite of everything we've been told.

The looks on the following pages are loud as hell. They're not for everyone, they're for us. We are not asking for your permission to exist, we're letting you know that we're here, we're irrepressible, and we're dancing.

We are making up for lost time.

***LOVING OURSELVES* defiantly, in spite of everything we've been told.**

ALANA, **SHANNON** (right), and **LINDY** (next) wear custom *MARK MITCHELL* Shout Your Abortion gowns. Photographed by *VICTORIA KOVIOS*.

I'm exhausted after a lifetime of men thinking they have the right to tell me what to do with my body.

Loving yourself is not antithetical to health, it is intrinsic to health. You can't take good care of a thing you hate.

WE ARE NOT ASKING FOR YOUR PERMISSION TO EXIST, ***we're letting you know that we're here, we're irrepressible, and we're dancing.***

ART BY **FRANK CORREA**

ABORTION
IS
PRO-LIFE
ABORTION
IS
PRO-LIFE

ART BY **FRANK CORREA**

EVERYONE
KNOWS
I HAD AN
ABORTION
EVERYONE
KNOWS
I HAD AN
ABORTION

ABORTION ♥ ABORTION ♥ ABORTION

ABORTION

Shout Your Abortion Forever

#Shout your abortion
flash by VALENTINE'S TATTOO CO.
oh bondage, UP YOURS!
NEVER AGAIN
ABORTION IS OK!
ABORTION
ask me about my abortion!
abortion is normal
DONT FUCKING TOUCH ME
ABORT SHAME
GOD ♡'S ABORTION
you dont own me
ABORTION IS NORMAL!
MEN DONT PROTECT YOU ANYMORE
abortion
abortion
MY BODY MY CHOICE
ABORTION IS OK!
MY BODY MY CHOICE!
SYA 206
ABORTION IS NORMAL
My Body
Abort Shame
shout your abortion
abortion
SYA
PRO ABORTION
PRO VASECTOMY
My Rules
matriarchy
ABORTION IS NORMAL
CRUSH THE PATRIARCHY

ERIN: Generally my tattoos don't have any specific meaning or significance—looking cool was always my main objective, and getting tattoos is fun. However, I NEVER would have gotten a tattoo with the word "abortion" a year ago *because* it would have felt too personally significant or serious. After talking about my abortions for the last year, getting this tattoo didn't feel like a big decision or heavy in any way. It's a cute tattoo and getting it felt normal, which I guess is the whole point.

JAY: Sometimes one of the most revolutionary and loving things we can do is to tell the truth in public. While my body owes the world nothing, it knows and (now) shouts this particular truth: abortion is normal!

LILA: By the power of the bold and beautiful poodle, I reject shame and all of its implications and injustices.

TATI: I don't know if I felt shame for my actual abortion, or more shame for the relationship I was in, and the person I was, prior to the abortion. I want to abort that shame, and no longer feel negative about the choices I've made that make me who I am today. Viva red lips!

BROOKE: This tattoo will be a daily reminder of why I'm committed to working in abortion care, even though it's so often difficult and fraught with strange challenges: my job allows me to empower other women, help keep them safe, and encourage them to trust themselves with a decision that only they can understand.

NEVER
AGAIN

DASH: Every day, strangers and friends read the words tattooed all over my arms and body with excitement. These words mean everything to me, and they tell a story that is not just my own.

With this "abortion is normal" tattoo, talking about abortion and womxn's rights will become an unavoidable, constant conversation in my life. The judgments and questioning I'll face going forward are nothing compared to the emotional, political, spiritual, and personal labor womxn go through every single day simply trying to exist. The least I can do is turn my skin into a small banner and join the fight for the freedom that womxn have deserved for all of herstory.

ABORTION
IS
NORMAL!

MOLLY: I grew up in a state that is hostile to abortion rights, and I continue to work in red states. The day I stop fighting for abortion rights is the day I die. When that day comes, I want everyone to know I was proud of my life's work.

abortion

AMELIA: It was either this or the knuckles!

ABORTION

REVERBERATION

what's past is prologue

WE ARE VOLCANOES. WHEN WE WOMEN OFFER OUR EXPERIENCE AS OUR TRUTH, AS HUMAN TRUTH, ALL THE MAPS CHANGE. THERE ARE NEW MOUNTAINS. –URSULA K. LE GUIN

New York, 1975.

New York, 1985.

New York, 1981.

New York, 1977.

Olympia, 1970.

Seattle, 1970.

Abortion
REFORM
NOW!
ABORTION
OR
BUST!
WOMEN
A CHOICE!

RESOURCES

CRISIS LINES

NATIONAL SUICIDE PREVENTION LIFELINE AND CRISIS CALL CENTER

https://suicidepreventionlifeline.org

Call 1-800-273-8255 or text "ANSWER" to 839863

The National Suicide Prevention Lifeline and the Crisis Call Center connect callers and texters with confidential support and local resources. These hotlines can be used by anyone, 24 hours a day, 7 days a week, and are useful for people in distress or crisis, people contemplating suicide, and anyone seeking crisis resources for themselves or others.

RAPE, ABUSE & INCEST NATIONAL NETWORK (RAINN)

National Sexual Assault Hotline: 1-800-656-HOPE (4673)

Chat online at https://online.rainn.org

Chat online in Spanish at https://online.rainn.org/es

RAINN is the country's largest anti-sexual violence organization. Call RAINN's National Sexual Assault Hotline or chat with RAINN online to be connected with a trained staff member from a sexual assault service provider in your area. The hotline and chat room give you access to a range of free services including confidential support, referrals to local health facilities that provide sexual assault services, referrals for long-term support, and legal information.

THE TREVOR PROJECT

https://thetrevorproject.org

The Trevor Lifeline: Call 1-866-488-7386 or text "TREVOR" to 1-202-304-1200

The Trevor Project is the leading national organization providing crisis intervention and suicide prevention services to lesbian, gay, bisexual, transgender and questioning (LGBTQ) young people ages 13–24.

ABORTION AND REPRODUCTIVE HEALTH CARE RESOURCES

ALL-OPTIONS PREGNANCY RESOURCE CENTER

https://all-options.org

All-Options Hotline: 1-888-493-0092

All-Options provides unconditional, judgment-free support for all your feelings, decisions, and experiences with pregnancy, parenting, abortion, and adoption. Call toll-free from anywhere in the United States and Canada, Monday through Friday from 10:00 a.m. to 1:00 a.m., and Saturday through Sunday from 10:00 a.m. to 6:00 p.m. (Eastern Time).

ABORTION CARE NETWORK (ACN)

https://abortioncarenetwork.org

ACN is the national association for independent, community-based abortion care providers and their allies. The ACN website has a nationwide list of independent abortion clinics and information about how to support your local indie providers.

NATIONAL ABORTION FEDERATION (NAF)

https://prochoice.org

Toll-free phone: 1-800-772-9100

The NAF Hotline Fund operates the largest national, toll-free, multilingual hotline for abortion referrals and financial assistance in the U.S. and Canada. NAF provides callers with accurate information, confidential consultation, options counseling, and referrals to providers of quality abortion care. They also provide case management services for women with special needs, and limited financial assistance to help subsidize care and travel-related expenses. The NAF hotline is free, completely anonymous, and offers services to everyone, regardless of their individual situation. Call for unbiased information about abortion and other resources, including financial assistance, Monday through Friday from 7:00 a.m. to 11:00 p.m., and Saturday through Sunday, 9:00 a.m. through 5:00 p.m. (Eastern Time).

For NAF referrals to quality abortion providers, call: 1-877-257-0012

Monday through Friday from 9:00 a.m. to 9:00 p.m., and Saturday through Sunday from 9:00 a.m. through 5:00 p.m. (Eastern Time). No funding assistance provided on this line.

NATIONAL NETWORK OF ABORTION FUNDS (NNAF)

https://abortionfunds.org

NNAF is a network of approximately 70 organizations that work at the intersections of racial, economic, and reproductive justice to remove financial and logistical barriers to abortion access. These organizations work with clinics to help pay for abortions and assist people having abortions with transportation, childcare, translation, doula services, and lodging. Visit the NNAF website to find out which resources are available in your state, and to learn more about how your donation to NNAF will directly support abortion access for people in need.

PLANNED PARENTHOOD

https://plannedparenthood.org

Call 1-800-230-PLAN (7526) to find a Planned Parenthood health center

Planned Parenthood is the largest single provider of reproductive and sexual health care in the U.S., and it engages in advocacy, education, and lobbying on behalf of reproductive rights. Each affiliate provides different services, which include STI testing, birth control, abortion, and emergency contraception.

THE WORLD PROFESSIONAL ASSOCIATION OF TRANSGENDER HEALTH (WPATH)

https://wpath.org

The World Professional Association for Transgender Health (WPATH) is a non-profit, interdisciplinary professional and educational organization devoted to transgender health. WPATH works to promote evidence based care, education, research, advocacy, public policy, and respect in transgender health. WPATH provides referrals to healthcare professionals as well as educational resources related to trans healthcare.

SELF-MANAGED ABORTION RESOURCES

MISOPROSTOL/MIFEPRISTONE

Misoprostol (alone or in combination with mifepristone) is a safe and effective way to end a pregnancy in the first 10 weeks and has been used successfully by millions of people all over the world without a clinician. The following organizations are well-vetted sources of information for those seeking to end an early pregnancy outside of a clinic setting, either because they lack access to legal abortion or simply want to manage their own abortions independently.

SELF-MANAGED ABORTION; SAFE AND SUPPORTED (SASS)

https://abortionpillinfo.org

Email: info@womenhelp.org

SASS is a support service that provides information and one-on-one support for those in the U.S. looking to end their own pregnancies. The site does not sell or issue abortion pills. SASS can connect you with experienced counselors who can help you decide whether you're a good candidate for self-managed abortion and offer medical referrals, and who are directly advised by OB-GYNs and experts on medication abortion.

PLAN C

https://plancpills.org

Plan C provides information to help people acquire abortion pills and safely use them. In 2017, Plan C ordered abortion pills from 14 websites without a prescription, and tested the pills they received. The test results are listed in a report card, which rates the reliability of the medication purchased on various websites, including information about pricing, shipping times, and amounts of active ingredients in the drugs received. Because these online pharmacy services are unregulated, there is no way to assess the authenticity or quality of the products these websites currently provide, but at the time of this writing there is no reason to suspect that the quality of pills from the sites reviewed on Plan C has changed.

LEGAL SUPPORT

Even though abortion is legal in the U.S., abortion pills are only legally available through abortion care providers. People who have medication abortions with pills ordered online through nonclinical channels may face unwarranted risk of arrest. The following organizations can provide support to people currently facing legal trouble surrounding a pregnancy or information for those who want to know how to protect themselves from being penalized by the government in pregnancy-related situations.

NATIONAL ADVOCATES FOR PREGNANT WOMEN (NAPW)

https://advocatesforpregnantwomen.org

Phone: 1-212-255-9252

NAPW is a nonprofit organization that works to secure the human and civil rights, health, and welfare of all people, focusing particularly on pregnant and parenting women, and those who are most likely to be targeted for state control and punishment—low-income women, women of color, and drug-using women.

THE SIA LEGAL TEAM

https://sialegalteam.org

Legal Helpline: 1-844-868-2812

Email: info@sialegalteam.org

SIA is working to transform the legal landscape so people can end their own pregnancies with dignity and without punishment.

FAQ

HOW DO I FIND SYA?

www.shoutyourabortion.com
ShoutYourAbortion@Gmail.com
@ShoutYrAbortion on Twitter
@ShoutYourAbortion on Instagram
@ShoutYourAbortionUSA on Facebook

IS SYA AN "OFFICIAL" ORGANIZATION OR WHAT?

Yes! After the hashtag blew up, Amelia started connecting with people all over the country and looking around for funding. After a few months of piecemeal donations, crowdfunding, and borrowing money from family members, SYA was able to secure a grant that got us off the ground and allowed us to start thinking about long-term strategy and start paying ourselves and others for their time. SYA has nonprofit sponsorship, meaning we function like a nonprofit and can accept tax-deductible donations, but we're also an LLC. At the time of this writing, SYA is in its third year as an organization, and we fund our programming with grants, donations, speaking fees, and income from our online shop. Our budget pays our tiny but mighty staff and allows us to make stuff like this book and facilitate projects and events all over the country.

SYA functions more like a collective than a traditional nonprofit. We are a loose, decentralized network of individuals who are talking about abortion on our own terms, and those terms are individually defined. We see SYA as a conduit. Each community that springs up around the concept of SYA is responsible for establishing their own values and norms. What works for a group of punks in Brooklyn will probably not work as well for a group of retirees in the Midwest—in fact, these groups might find one another's tone or tactics questionable!—and that's okay. In fact, that's great! SYA believes that the effort to dismantle compulsory silence and shame surrounding abortion requires a vast range of approaches. You do you.

CAN I BE A PART OF SYA? HOW DO I DO IT?

Congratulations! Your application has been accepted and you are now an official SYA operative. As far as how to do it, you can find ideas in this book, you can visit our website and sign up for our newsletter (which we use to send out various calls for participation), and you can follow us on social media for additional ideas and inspiration. You can add your abortion story to our Webby Award–winning website, via text, video, or photograph, anonymously or not. You can go to our website and read other people's abortion stories and then talk about them or share them with the people in your life. You can pass this book along to someone else when you're done with it, or you can buy everyone you love their very own copy.

You can also just do your own thing altogether. Some things that people have done include: making zines, having art shows, writing love letters to abortion clinics, organizing a book club, having a film screening, producing a storytelling or comedy event, having a button-making party, painting a mural, hanging a banner on an overpass, writing songs about abortion, making music videos or podcasts about abortion, students doing research projects about abortion and abortion stigma, putting together a panel discussion with community organizations that work on abortion-related issues, hosting an abortion speak-out, telling someone or everyone about your abortion, talking about abortion on a first date, talking about abortion with a child, letting the people in your life know that you want to support them if and when they have abortions, throwing yourself or your loved one a party to honor, celebrate, grieve, or otherwise commemorate a recent or upcoming abortion.

WHERE ARE YOU LOCATED? IS SYA A U.S.-FOCUSED ORGANIZATION?

SYA has no official headquarters. Our work is focused in the U.S., although we do have friends and sister organizations in other countries (*Kochamy cię Aborcyjny Dream Team!*) and we support universal access to abortion without shame for everyone in the universe.

HOW SHOULD I DEAL WITH THE POSSIBILITY OF ANTI-CHOICE PROTESTERS AT AN EVENT I'M PLANNING?

Dozens of SYA events have happened all over the country without anti-choice people showing up, but sometimes they do. Prepare for the possibility by setting aside time before your event and checking in with event hosts and volunteers. Considerations about security vary based on where you live, whether your event is public or private, the size and nature of the event, the venue, and the resources available to you. Because of all those variables, it's difficult for us to advise you specifically on what your game plan should be. We suggest discussing what your system of responses will be if anti-choice people show up, based on their tactics and how uncomfortable they are making you feel. For example, your group might decide that a couple of people holding anti-choice signs outside of the venue doesn't merit any response, but that if one of them tries to come inside, you will deny them entry. You might also decide that if a group of protesters becomes more vocal and is harassing attendees or encroaching on private property, you will call law enforcement or campus security, or you may agree not to involve these groups. You may decide to hire professional security for your event or enlist a door person from your favorite bar. We believe in your ability to decide what feels right and reasonable based on your unique situation. If someone is making you or your guests feel unsafe, you have every right to treat that threat as serious and use whatever resources you would normally use to report a threatening person: telling them, "You are harassing me," "You are making me feel unsafe," "I need you to stop threatening people and leave," or "I'm calling security." And then call for help (the owner of the venue, a mentor, security, or 911 if you wish). We recommend deciding which resource you will call in advance and talking about that with your team so you're not scrambling for a number in the moment.

As much as SYA absolutely believes that anti-choice protesters should be met with resistance, we can't in good conscience recommend engaging with them. We generally treat them like we don't even see them. Their goal is to terrorize us, and our indifference is their failure. Whatever you decide to do, remember that you don't owe them a drop of your energy. Anti-choice protesters are a human comment section. Don't waste your light.

HOW DO YOU DEAL WITH ONLINE TROLLS AND WHAT ADVICE DO YOU HAVE FOR PEOPLE WHO ARE EXPERIENCING ONLINE HARASSMENT?

When people harass us online, we delete their comments and block them immediately. There is an incredible wealth of information and resources about online harassment at www.crashoverridenetwork.com. There is also an excellent toolkit at https://onlinesafety.feministfrequency.com, which was created by activists Anita Sarkeesian, Jaclyn Friedman, and Renee Bracey Sherman. It outlines some quick, easy precautions that are geared toward protecting people who may be more vulnerable to harassment as members of a marginalized group or because they are engaging in online activism. We highly recommend taking a look at these sites before sharing your abortion story publicly, and they're good resources for everybody who uses the internet.

CAN I USE YOUR LOGO?

Probably! Email us a little more information. We might also be able to help promote your event/action/art through our website, newsletter, or social media.

CAN I USE YOUR MESSAGING?

Please do! SYA messaging belongs to everyone and it's meant to be widely proliferated.

CAN I RIP OFF ONE OF YOUR T-SHIRTS?

Buying things from our website is essentially donating to SYA because the revenue goes right back into our programs. But if you'd prefer to make your own abortion-related swag that is inspired by ours, that's great too! We're flattered. Obviously it would be weird if you acted like one of our ideas was your idea or you used one of our ideas to make money without talking to us, so please don't be weird like that. And because our stuff is mostly made by individual artists who have their own particulars about how people use their work, you should ask us if you want to replicate something and we will ask the artist.

I HAVE A GREAT IDEA FOR AN SYA EVENT! CAN YOU HELP ME WITH RESOURCES AND FUNDING?

Maybe! Email us to tell us more about what you have in mind and join our mailing list to receive our calls for events.

CAN YOU SPEAK AT / HAVE A TABLE AT MY EVENT?

We are available as schedules allow, sometimes for a modest fee.

DO YOU DONATE MERCH TO GOOD CAUSES?

Often! If you have a silent auction or raffle coming up to support your org, hit us up!

CAN I DONATE TO SYA?

Yes, thanks! As a nonprofit project, we can accept tax-deductible gifts of service, goods, or cold, hard cash, which we use to support all sorts of projects, art commissions, and events. You can donate via our website.

CREDITS & NOTES

FOREWORD, PREFACE

Pages viii, xi: art by Jolene Barnes

FORMATION

Pages 1, 4–5: art by Emily Nokes

INTRODUCTION: ORGANIZATION

Page 6: clockwise from upper left: zines made by Shout Your Abortion Brooklyn, button-making party photos by SYA, Chop Suey photos by Victoria Holt
Page 7: top: photo by Kelly O; bottom: photo by SYA

SHOUTS

Page 13: art by Emily Nokes
Page 17: art by Erin Jorgensen
Page 19: photo courtesy of Lesley Hazleton
Page 20: photo by Jenny Jimenez
Page 23: necklace by SYA (available at shoutyourabortion.com)
Page 27: art by Maggie Prendergast
Page 28: photo by Jesse Booher
Page 31: art by Mary Anne Carter
Page 39: mural by Ezra Dickinson, photo by Kelly O
Page 45: poem by Michael McKinney
Page 48, top: photo by Elliot Luscombe; bottom: photo by Viva Ruiz; right: photo by Santiago Felipe
Page 50: photo by Niffer Calderwood
Page 52: photo courtesy of Amy Brenneman
Page 55: photo by SYA
Page 59: photo by Erin Jorgensen
Page 65: art by Tyler Bosch
Page 66: photo by Ian Allen
Page 73: photo by SYA / Kelly O
Page 81: art by Kirk Damer
Page 85: art by Dana Davenport
Page 86: photo courtesy of Wendy Davis
Page 89: art by Coco Howard
Page 95: photo by SYA
Page 101: art by Tyler Bosch
Page 107: cake by Erin Jorgensen
Page 109: photo by anonymous
Page 111: poem by Lila Bonow
Page 121: art by Tara Thomas
Page 122: photo by Ted Zee
Page 124: poster by Andrew Lamb
Page 125: clockwise from top: photo by Ted Zee, photo by Ted Zee, photo by Tatiana Gill, photo of DoNormaal by Victoria Holt, photo by Kelly O
Page 129: art by Leigh Riibe
Page 133: art by Caitlin Blunnie
Page 149: art by Christopher Harrell
Page 153: art by Jen Corace
Pages 170–171: art by Doug Newman

Photographer Elizabeth Rudge travelled to Seattle, Los Angeles, Houston, Austin, Memphis, Washington DC, Philadelphia, and New York City in order to shoot the majority of the storytellers featured in the Shouts section in their home cities. Elizabeth's commitment to this project and to her subjects brought this book to life, and we are very grateful. Elizabeth's portraits appear throughout the Shouts [essays] section, pages 13–153, unless otherwise indicated.

PROVIDERS

Page 173: art by Emily Nokes
Pages 176–183: illustrations by Kathryn Rathke

INSPIRATION

Page 185: art by Emily Nokes
Pages 186–187: photos by SYA
Pages 188–189: photos by Kelly O
Page 190: photo by Holly Calvasina
Pages 191–192, 194–195: posters and photos by Civilization
Page 193: photo by Victoria Holt, *Abortion is Freedom* poster by Emily Nokes, held by Sarah Stokes
Pages 196–197: photos by Kelly O
Pages 198–199: photo by Jackie Neale, copyright 2016
Pages 200–201, 206–207: photos by Ben Sellon
Page 208: essay by Amelia Bonow
Pages 202–203: photos by The Illuminator
Pages 204–205: photos by Kathy Armstrong

NOTES ON BUTTONS

The button templates in this section are all available for free download on our website. Button makers are a few hundred bucks, but you may know a friendly organization or band that has one you could borrow, and there are plenty of online vendors that will make buttons for you.

NOTES ON POSTERS

The poster templates in this section are available for free download on our website. Carry one to a rally, or put some up in your neighborhood! Just make sure you research whether or not postering is legal at the spot you have in mind.

NOTES ON PROJECTIONS

We've got a number of reels on our website that can be streamed from your computer through a projector or onto any TV with an HDMI port. We've done a lot of this with our friends at The Illuminator—check out http://theilluminator.org/tools for tips on getting started.

FASHION

Page 209: *Abortion is Normal* purse by Michele Pred for SYA
Pages 214–215: models, clockwise from top left: Kim Selling, Frank Correa, Adé, Elvia Carreon
Page 216–217: models, clockwise from top left: Kelly O, Saige Leah, anonymous, Emily Wolf
Page 218: photo of Kierra Johnson by Tawni Bannister for *BUST*, in gown by Jordan Christianson with fabric printed by Ink Knife Press
Page 219: photo of Shannon Perry by Tawni Bannister for *BUST*, necklace by SYA, clothing model's own
Pages 220–225: photos by Kelly O; tattoos by Valentine's Tattoo, including work by Shannon Perry, MKNZ Porritt, Albie, Dane, Lolli, and Johnathan Fleming

REVERBERATION

Page 227: art by Emily Nokes
Pages 228–231: photo by Bettye Lane, courtesy of *Schlesinger Library, Radcliffe Institute, Harvard University*
Page 232–233, left: photo by Joseph Karpen, courtesy of University of Washington, 1191, Joseph Karpen Collection; right: photo by Timothy Eagan, courtesy of MOHAI, Seattle Post-Intelligencer Collection, 1986.5.53075
Page 237: photo of Mindie Lind by SYA

ACKNOWLEDGMENTS

SYA has been built and sustained by a vast network of people, cobbling together skills and resources in order to make things happen. We've decided to skip general acknowledgments because there are simply far to many people to thank, but we would like to thank the people who donated their time in order to help us create this book. Our copywriters, fact checkers, and photo wizards are: Suzie Strait, Elli Cummins, Jeanne Gervais, Kelly O, Kevin Wren, and Civilization. And to our storytellers: thank you for trusting us. You are everything.

SYA is grateful for the grant we received from Abortion Conversation Projects, which will allow us to send subsidized books to dozens of abortion clinics for their waiting and recovery rooms. If you are clinic staff and would like to inquire about a subsidized book, please email shoutyourabortion@gmail.com.

SYA's staff is Amelia Bonow, Sara Edwards, and Erin Jorgensen.

\+ + +

ERIN JORGENSEN is a musician living in Seattle who has had four abortions and is doing great. She does part-time communications for SYA and helped produce this book by taking photos, organizing things, showing up in many different scenarios and doing what needed to be done, and dropping a banner off an overpass the day Justice Kennedy announced his retirement.

SARA EDWARDS is an American artist pursuing freedom and self-reliance while living in the high Rocky Mountains with her dog Michael Jackson. She is the codirector of SYA and helped make this book happen by collecting more than a hundred waivers, drafting dozens of contracts and processing more than seventy-five contributor invoices, and triple-checking countless things that nobody else would have checked.

SYA cofounder **LINDY WEST** is a *New York Times* columnist and the author of bestselling memoir and soon-to-be TV show, *Shrill*. Lindy has been part of countless conversations that have informed this book and the movement at large, and she has been endlessly encouraging. Having Lindy believe in you is very powerful because she is right about everything!

EMILY NOKES is a writer, graphic designer, Libra, singer in a band called Tacocat, and music editor at *BUST* magazine. Emily came onto this project as a book designer and coeditor, which ended up meaning that she spent *many* hours talking to Amelia and then somehow managed to turn all those conversations into the book that you are holding. From pixel wizardry to curation to overall vision, Emily did a whole lot of everything.

SYA cofounder and codirector **AMELIA BONOW** loves abortion care providers, dancing, making out, laughing at people but not in a mean way, talking about feelings, and watching her friends excel. Amelia had the overall idea for the book and then amassed a team capable of bringing it to life. She is grateful for every single person who has supported SYA, including you.

ABOUT PM PRESS

PM Press was founded at the end of 2007 by a small collection of folks with decades of publishing, media, and organizing experience. PM Press co-conspirators have published and distributed hundreds of books, pamphlets, CDs, and DVDs. Members of PM have founded enduring book fairs, spearheaded victorious tenant organizing campaigns, and worked closely with bookstores, academic conferences, and even rock bands to deliver political and challenging ideas to all walks of life. We're old enough to know what we're doing and young enough to know what's at stake.

We create radical and stimulating fiction and non-fiction books, pamphlets, T-shirts, visual and audio materials to entertain, educate, and inspire you. We aim to distribute these through every available channel with every available technology—whether that means you are seeing anarchist classics at our book fair stalls, reading our latest vegan cookbook at the café, downloading geeky fiction e-books, or digging new music and timely videos from our website. PM Press is always on the lookout for talented and skilled volunteers, artists, activists, and writers to work with.

If you have a great idea for a project or can contribute in some way, please get in touch.

PM Press
PO Box 23912
Oakland, CA 94623
www.pmpress.org

ABOUT BETWEEN THE LINES

Founded in 1977, Between the Lines publishes books that support social change and justice. Our goal is not private gain, nor are we owned by a faceless conglomerate. We are cooperatively run by our employees and a small band of volunteers who share a tenacious belief in books, authors, and ideas that break new ground.

Between the Lines books present new ideas and challenge readers to rethink the world around them. Our authors offer analysis of historical events and contemporary issues not often found in the mainstream. We specialize in informative, non-fiction books on politics and public policy, social issues, history, international development, gender and sexuality, critical race issues, culture, adult and popular education, labour and work, environment, technology, and media.

"Who is your leader?"

We create high-quality books that promote equitable social change, and we reflect our mission in the way our organization is structured. BTL has no bosses, no owners. It's the product of what some would likely describe as "sixties idealism"—what we call political principles. Our small office staff and Editorial Committee make decisions—from what to publish to how to run the place—by consensus. Our Editorial Committee includes a number of original and long-time members, as well as several younger academics and community activists eager to carry on the publishing work started by the generation before them.

www.btlbooks.com

FRIENDS OF PM

These are indisputably momentous times—the financial system is melting down globally and the Empire is stumbling. Now more than ever there is a vital need for radical ideas. In the years since its founding—and on a mere shoestring—PM Press has risen to the formidable challenge of publishing and distributing knowledge and entertainment for the struggles ahead. With over 400 releases to date, we have published an impressive and stimulating array of literature, art, music, politics, and culture. Using every available medium, we've succeeded in connecting those hungry for ideas and information to those putting them into practice.

Friends of PM allows you to directly help impact, amplify, and revitalize the discourse and actions of radical writers, filmmakers, and artists. It provides us with a stable foundation from which we can build upon our early successes and provides a much-needed subsidy for the materials that can't necessarily pay their own way. You can help make that happen—and receive every new title automatically delivered to your door once a month—by joining as a Friend of PM Press. And, we'll throw in a free T-shirt when you sign up.

Here are your options:

- **$30 a month** Get all books and pamphlets plus 50% discount on all webstore purchases
- **$40 a month** Get all PM Press releases (including CDs and DVDs) plus 50% discount on all webstore purchases
- **$100 a month** Superstar—Everything plus PM merchandise, free downloads, and 50% discount on all webstore purchases
- **$15 a month** eBooks—Get all eBooks plus 50% discount on all webstore purchases

For those who can't afford $30 or more a month, we have **Sustainer Rates** at $15, $10, and $5. Sustainers get a free PM Press T-shirt and a 50% discount on all purchases from our website.

Your Visa or Mastercard will be billed once a month, until you tell us to stop. Or until our efforts succeed in bringing the revolution around. Or the financial meltdown of Capital makes plastic redundant. Whichever comes first.

Sign up at www.pmpress.org